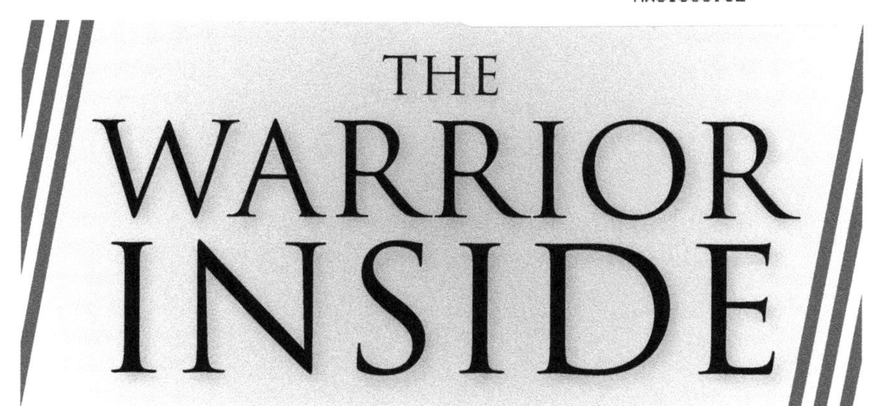

JEANETTE GOLDEN

and

CHARLENE MAXFIELD

ISBN 978-1-64458-821-5 (paperback)
ISBN 978-1-64458-822-2 (digital)

Christian Faith Publishing, Inc.
832 Park Avenue
Meadville, PA 16335
www.christianfaithpublishing.com

Printed in the United States of America

DEDICATION

I dedicate this book to my adoptive parents, Richard and Barbara Kurtz, as well as my adoptive sister, Terri, and my adoptive brother, Kevin. Had it not been for them, this book would never have been written.

Psalm 27:10 (King James Version) reads,

> When my father and mother forsake me,
> then the Lord will take me up.

During the dark and fearful years of my life, God sent to me the most precious family anyone could ever ask for. The Kurtzes adopted me, a kid off the street with a blemished past. Yet they loved me unconditionally. My adoptive siblings also accepted me without reservation. Never was I made to feel like the black sheep in the family. I truly was a daughter and sister to this beloved family. It is a miracle that changed my life forever.

The Kurtzes are the most loving, generous, gracious, and unselfish people I have ever known. There are not enough words in the dictionary to express the love and appreciations I have for them.

I want to thank each of them, including the extended family, for leaving me the greatest legacy of all: that of loving others as Jesus loves them.

I also want to dedicate this book to my precious husband, Gary. He is the love of my life and my best friend. He has loved me without question throughout our thirty-six years of marriage. He has been a hard worker and a faithful provider. I could not fulfil God's purpose in my life without his love, sacrifice, and support.

In dedicating this book I could not leave out one of the greatest blessings in my life, my children and grandchildren, Rob, Kurt and Drew, Easton, Gauge and Magnolia. My heart overflows with gratefulness for the beautiful family God has provided. I am blessed beyond measure.

Adoptive Parents Mom Barbara and Dad Richard

CONTENTS

ACKNOWLEDGMENTS

To my dear friend, Charlene Maxfield, I would like to say thank you for the tireless hours you spent writing this book. I came to you, holding back nothing as I shared my story. What could have been a dry, tragic melodrama was transformed into a masterful work of art. You used your wit, humor, and God-given abilities to make this book not only an enjoyable read, but a tool to be used to help those who have had similar experiences as me. My heart's cry was to reach the hurting and the lost. You have made my vision complete. You're awesome, girl!

CHAPTER 1

GHOSTS OF THE PAST

In the moonlight, I could see vague distant figures wafting through the air. Seemingly transparent, I watched them advance in the direction of my hiding place. A chill ran down my spine despite the sweltering summer night air. Beads of perspiration covered my forehead like a blanket. My palms were clammy and trembling.

As the crazed apparitions ran through the woods, tree branches whipped to and fro, slicing through the humidity. The twigs on the ground were crushed into a fine powder, floating through the air as the heavy footsteps of the phantom ghosts trampled the ground underfoot. I could feel the trembling of the earth beneath me as it became apparent they were coming for me.

I stood like a statue frozen in time, afraid to breathe. I was terrified that I would be discovered. My heart raced as they drew closer. Suddenly, silence fell all around me, and I saw them in clear view. In all their translucent fury, they rushed toward me. Their eyes were filled with flames of fire and sharp daggers. They looked menacing and violent. Their voices were filled with hatred and rage. Blasphemous words spewed from their mouths like erupting volcanoes. All in unison they began to chant, "Thief! Harlot! Liar!" They spat words at me like venom. The words tore through me like knives as they began to circle around where I now lay helpless on the dirt-filled ground.

I squeezed my eyes tightly, bracing myself for the impact of their thrashing words. My back began to sting from what felt like broken glass shattering beneath me. A scream ripped through me, mercifully waking me from the nightmare and dispelling the frightening vision. Relief washed over me as I realized the encounter with these horrid beasts was not real. It had been yet another of many tormenting dreams. These dreams seemed to be intruding ever more frequently, as if to make a home inside my mind.

I was once told that the nightmares I was plagued with were due to the trauma of my younger years. I learned the subconscious mind could bring ghosts from the past into my world at the most unexpected times. They claw their way up through the ground floor of your mind, rearing their ugly heads. They take advantage of you when you are most vulnerable, such as when you are sleeping. Whether these terrifying experiences are real or a dream, they can result in anxiety, panic, and even phobias. The mind can bring up past events you thought were long forgotten.

Although portions of the brain serve as shock absorbers, they work to generate a cushion for the mind to prevent overload. This creates a coping mechanism through which your brain funnels horrifying experiences in such a way as if to sift through the traumatic effect. Many times, these memories will be unearthed when you least expect them. They may come to light when you are more equipped to handle them. This process may take months or years before memories finally surface.

My siblings and I were certainly familiar with traumatic memories. We lived in a world filled with uncertainties, fear, abuse, and poverty. We existed in a world where stealing was a means to eat. Often, we were forced into the streets to find shelter when we could not pay for rent. Our stepfather squandered all his money on liquor. Day-to-day life was a frightening existence filled with unwelcome surprises that became seemingly worse as time passed.

Our reality was enough to send any adult running for the hills. Looking back makes it difficult to comprehend. As children, it was nearly impossible to wrap our brains around what was happening in our home. We simply fought to keep our heads above water. At times, I felt as though these attempts were futile, like I was going to drown.

In my small world, there were murders, rapes, incest, and beatings, some of which I witnessed myself. We were living in a war zone filled with constant explosions of despicable events, followed by hopes of a better tomorrow. Unfortunately, those hopes were then blown into tiny unrecognizable pieces.

It took me years to realize the full impact of how the events of my past truly affected me. They left me with a view of the world that was never meant to be seen. It brought fears that should never have been. In many ways, your childhood shapes you and molds you into the person you will become as an adult.

Mercifully, I did not choose to rehearse the same song and verse of my life's melodramatic orchestration. Instead, I chose to throw it out altogether. I decided to sing a new song, drafting a sweet symphony of love, joy, and peace. This process did not take place overnight. For many years of my youth, I attempted to compartmentalize my life. I began to separate the old and the new and not mix them for fear it would interfere with this new world. I desired a world where I was no longer a victim of circumstance. I refused to talk about, or even think about, such vile things. I kept those memories at bay, locked away, out of sight and out of mind. Recalling those memories is somewhat like looking through tightly spun cobwebs that surround events of my life I was reluctant to uncover.

Beginning at an early age, I felt trapped in those cobwebs. I was like the prey of a spider just waiting to be devoured. There were only two choices: to claw my way out with every fiber of my being or fall victim to the spinning unseen spider stalking my every move. I chose to fight my way out. I found within me a reserve of strength, and I decided to put it into full force. I was unable to control the situation, but I certainly was not going to allow it to control me. I found the courage to fight my way out, knowing I would be leaving the rest of my family behind. I felt at times I was leaving them in a putrefying rot and dooming peril that was sure to befall them. But I did not have the strength to carry them out with me. As I made my way out with terrifying struggle, their faces began to fade away like dust in an abandoned desert. The cobwebs themselves seemed out of reach. I knew death would certainly overtake me if I fell short of safer grounds. I had hoped they had the strength to follow, but as I turned in hopes of seeing them, I saw instead only dead space around me. A chill swept across my body as I left with the realization that I would be taking this journey alone. Later, I would find that I was never alone.

To understand my pursuit to safer grounds, perhaps I should share the beginning of my story. I was born in Canton, Georgia, on August 28, 1960. In my family were nine children. I had two older sisters and six brothers. When I was a baby, my father, Hershel, was murdered in a truck explosion. When he turned on the ignition, the truck exploded, and my father died instantly. My two cousins were in the truck with him at the time of the explosion. Unfortunately, they were also victims of this horrific crime. There was little investigation done after the murders, and the person or people responsible for the deaths were never found. Rumors pointed to the very man that became my stepfather soon after my father's death. My stepfather was already a part of our family for he was my mother's first cousin. He never faced criminal charges in the case.

My mind often wanders in search of what my biological father was like and how my life would have been different had he lived. Although I did not have the opportunity to know my biological father, I was told that he was a very kind, gentle, and loving man. I am certain my story would have been much different had I spent my life with him rather than the one I bring to you now.

The devil comes in many different disguises. To save time, I will sum up the description of my stepfather with a passage in the Bible.

John 10:10 (King James Version) reads,

> The thief cometh not, but for to steal, and to kill, and to destroy.

From my perspective, my stepfather was the devil manifested inside of a human vessel. I truly felt as though I was living with Satan himself. Hand him a pitchfork, and he would be dressed for the occasion. At times, I fully expected him to sprout horns. He was a true born chameleon. With military precision, he would clothe himself in the camouflage of a father's love. He would then set out to achieve his mission. He would slide like a snake into my bedroom in the night to torment me in the darkness. Snakes are nocturnal creatures. They creep upon their prey, which are completely unaware of the serpent's presence. The innocent victim is hit before they know it. My stepfather was the snake in the darkness as he held me in his grip. I felt as though I would smother.

To me, as a small child, he always looked like an ominous mass of evil. He would hover over my bed where I lay, pretending to be asleep. I always hoped that he would lose interest and leave, but that thought was always futile. His eyes would glare in my direction, as if he was trying to seduce me. He would tell me to take off my clothes. He would slide his callused hands up and down my body. My skin would redden from the touch of his sandpaper-like palms. Left behind were humiliating streaks that lingered, a cold reminder of the utter hell I lived in. These painful tattoos were a tormenting reminder of my reality. I can still feel the rawness of my skin and remember the helplessness and hopelessness that stole away my innocence. His heavy panting would steal away the silence in the room as he slid his hands from place to place, exploring my body. Sometimes, he would force me to perform oral sex until he reached some bizarre satisfaction. Many times, I felt as though I was stuck in a thick hole of quicksand. The more I struggled and tried to escape, the more it would pull me further and further in. This was so disgusting and humiliating to me, it would literally make me ill. Sometimes I would feel like passing out.

He was the monster I was running from in my nightmares. My life felt as though I was in a tornado, with debris flying all around me. I was trapped in the vortex of the tornadic winds of my life. At times, I would find myself envious of Dorothy in the Wizard of Oz, wishing that I, too, could be swept far away to a magical land where nothing bad happens and then fall asleep peacefully in a field of beautiful flowers. But I was all too aware this only happens in the movies.

When the devil was finished with me, he would whisper in my ear with a snake-like hiss. His words would be filled with threats, forcing me to secrecy. As tears filled my eyes, he would hiss, "Big girls don't cry." At the time, he forced me to believe I was big and that keeping a secret of this magnitude showed some sort of mature responsibility on my part. However, the truth of the matter was that I was not a big girl. I was a little girl, not even fully developed yet. It was as if I was left in the middle of a horrendous battlefield, ravaged and left for ruin.

Eventually my stepfather would tire of me and leave me to myself. Once alone in my bed, a torrent of tears would make their way down my cheeks and gratitude would welcome me into their warm embrace. I had paid my dues one more night living as a Jones.

Mornings at my home did not include waking up to coffee brewing, eggs scrambling, bacon sizzling, or joyful laughing to welcome a new day. Instead, I was greeted by my stepfather, ordering me not to shame myself by shining light on what was happening between him, me, and my sisters. He was a clever monster, projecting his guilt onto me, as if I had done something wrong. He was a master manipulator. He was able to make things appear as if the problem fell on me and my sisters, and we were simply facing the consequences.

The devil continued to make his rounds and never ceased. Perhaps it would have been easier if he would have pinned a note to my pillow with date and time of our little meetings in the dark so that I would be more prepared. In truth, there was no way to prepare for the damage this monster inflicted upon me. As I watched him gloat in the charade of his arrogance, I cringed at the thought of calling him my father.

My stepfather had many punishing tactics when I did not do as he wished. And sometimes, he simply claimed displeasure, so he could punish me. Many times, I was ordered to unclothe, and he would whip me with a light cord, leaving welts up and down my body. As if that weren't enough, he would engage in making me sing to him in the nude to humiliate me.

Out of the corner of my eye, I would see my mother in the shadows, looking on as he had his way with me and my sisters. When my stepfather would see her, he would order her out of the room. She would quickly do as she was told or she herself would suffer the consequences. When the show was over, my mother was ordered to take issue with me and discipline me further. She always followed suit—out of fear, I assume.

I can recall on different occasions, he would place all of us in a circle, parade around us, chest puffed out and gun in hand. He would then point the gun to each of our heads and threaten to kill us. We all stood there, beyond petrified, and afraid this was our last time on planet earth. I trembled as he walked past me, closing my eyes to escape this living nightmare. There was no escaping. I could not move. I was at his mercy. We all were. *What if he shoots me and I die today? What if he shoots my sisters or brothers?* I was living a real nightmare in my own home. When his rant was over, I fell to the floor in relief that I could live one more day. Funny thing is, I was not sure if living was a blessing or a curse.

Growing up, it was clear that my family was dysfunctional. There were never words of kindness, only threats. My innocence was lost at a very young age. I supposed there would be no way of getting it back. It was a gift given to me in my youth and taken away by my stepfather before I could celebrate my teenage years.

At night, I would pull the covers up over my head to find some comfort. There were no dolls or teddy bears, no companions to snuggle up with. I dreamed about having a doll or teddy bear to hold. I guess as a child I thought if I had one to cuddle it would help to bring a comforting, calming, and tranquilizing effect to my emotions. However, cute and cuddly dolls cannot talk to you, wrap their arms around you, nor can they take on your emotional or physical pain. They can do nothing but stare blankly. If I had been allowed such a pleasure, I could have at least talked to my doll, knowing that she would never reveal my secrets.

In all my loneliness, my thoughts would often drift to stories I had heard. They were loving stories of mothers tucking their children into bed, reading them books until their eyes grew tired, and wooing them to sleep. Of course, this was never my story, but I found if I thought about such stories long enough, I could steal a bit of comfort knowing someone somewhere was living in this reality. Some would be waking to find their mothers in the kitchen preparing waffles and fresh juice, cartoons in the background, a loving father reading the newspaper. Such tales seemed a difficult concept for me to understand.

Most nights even these fantasies did not work to remove the sting of reality. Each night I hoped the next day would bring a miracle or a savior to take me out of this place. Each morning was a bitter disappointment as I woke to find myself amid a living hell once more.

I was forced to live one more day in a combat zone, ill-equipped to fight, and still somehow survive. I am aware, as I was then, that life is full of disappointments. I understand that well today. I have found that suffering harm from such a prominent figure in one's life at such an early age can be a debilitating injury, one that is near impossible to recover. People's words, actions, and deeds toward you shape your life and form your perspective about yourself.

I was living with the constant terror of what was coming down the pike next. I became hardened of heart, trusting no one and filled with an emptiness that can only be described as a black hole. Every child deserves to have a childhood filled with innocence and laughter, love, protection, and a worry-free world of imagination and joy.

Such a concept was out of reach from where I stood. It was simply unattainable. Our home was being run by the devil masquerading as my stepfather. He did just that, forgetting nothing and holding nothing back.

It is difficult to comprehend how life can be so altered by the very person who should be protecting you. Every little girl has the right to love her dad and be loved by him in a proper way. There should have been protection and shelter in my home. There was none.

Home sweet home should be a place that represents safety and love yet did not exist where I lived. I knew I was a survivor, and this is the thought that gave me hope and made me believe that I would overcome the ghosts of my past.

The Devil in Disguise

Truck Explosion Left Several Dead-Believed to Be Murdered

My Biological Father Who I Never Had the Chance to Meet

CHAPTER 2

ROBIN HOOD AND HIS MERRY MEN

Robin Hood was a heroic outlaw in English folklore. He was a highly skilled archer and swordsman. He was known for robbing from the rich and giving to the poor. He was assisted by a group of fellow outlaws known as his Merry Men.

My life of crime began at the ripe old age of seven when I accomplished my first heist. Before this, my mother crafted flowers out of wood fiber and toilet paper. These creations were then sold as corsages. We would sell them for fifty cents each to pay for just enough food to drag us through until the next grueling day.

There were days we were unable to sell any of our crafted flowers. If we couldn't sell, we couldn't eat. I don't recall many home-cooked meals growing up, to say the least. Often the only things in the kitchen were old cans of vegetables and a random assortment of stale condiments. I found that mixing ketchup and a can of veggies made a mixture resembling soup. Survival was of upmost importance!

I wouldn't dare say I was a chef, but I got the job done when food was scarce. I managed to come up with countless imaginative recipes. I rummaged through the sparse food resources in our cupboards and refrigerator to create a "gourmet" meal, or at least something edible. In our house, many times it was either get creative or starve.

Each day after school we would take to the streets in an effort to sell our next batch of my mother's homemade flowers. On many of these occasions, my mother would drop me off at a grungy, smoke-filled bar. Those holes-in-the-wall were referred to as honky-tonks. I still hold the image in my mind of my first run-through in such a bar.

I can still smell the pungent smells of alcohol, smoke, workmen's sweat, and women's overpowering perfume wafting through the air. The stench of it all burned my nostrils and my eyes as I made my way through the smoky fog. The windows were covered by tattered, sunburnt pieces of cloth to blot out the light. A tremor ran through my body as I pushed forward. My home was no paradise and a far cry from safe, but at home I knew what to expect. These places were unknown, uncharted territories.

I could not allow my fast beating heart and nervousness to give me away. I was frightened but had to put on a front of confidence and courage. Drunken men slumped over the bar with burning cigarettes hanging from their mouths. They looked unhappily in my direction. Their eyes peered down at me without even a hint of a smile playing across their lips. Sticky residue and ashes seemed to blanket everything.

I could almost hear the fear coursing through my veins. The music seemed to shake my very insides, but I knew I had to push through the terror in order for us to eat. I was aggressive as I made my way through the clusters of scowling faces.

Giving nothing away, I refused to allow them to sense my fear. Many did not notice the small child with stringy hair hanging in her face wandering through the bar. The ones who did notice made no effort to acknowledge me as they could see I was attempting to collect money by selling mother's homemade wares.

Others just glared in my direction, threatening me with their eyes. The bottoms of my shoes sunk into the floor like quicksand as I made my way through the globs of spilled drinks, used tobacco butts, and God only knows what. I felt if I didn't keep moving and stood idle the floors might swallow me up.

One by one I began to approach each of the customers with my rehearsed lines. Sadly, these lines were not a fabrication, but simply the CliffsNotes to a much larger tale of despair. My lines read something like this: "Our father was murdered in a tragic explosion, and I am trying to help my mother make a living. She has nine kids to support, and we have no food."

In truth, we had little because my stepfather was a drunk and a coward. He was also exceedingly lazy. Although when he did work, he drove what us kids called a "shit-truck" because he cleaned out septic tanks. He would also take my mother's social security checks and our child welfare checks and cash them to support his drinking habit, leaving us with nothing. Many times, we were forced to become homeless, living in cars, churches, and any means of shelter became a recurring theme for survival.

The start of my street hustling was a slow one. Very few people wanted these handmade corsages but bought them out of sympathy. They couldn't turn down a begging child. As charming as I'm sure I was, I just couldn't seem to swing it.

I would find a taker here and there, but often I came home empty-handed. I learned very quickly that an unsuccessful sales day equaled a heavy beating from my brother Chase. The thought of going hungry gave me the incentive to keep me moving forward. Ruling by fear was the way my family operated.

Chase held nothing back and was sure to remind me that beatings would be my reward each time I showed up empty-handed. At such a young age, I'm certain my sales ability lacked enthusiasm, and my product was less than desirable. I knew that I had to find a way to bring home the bacon; otherwise, this little dog-and-pony show was only going to get worse.

This is what led me to my first heist. I was growing increasingly tired of the beatings. The heavy despair was beginning to weigh on me. One afternoon at school there was a fund-raiser going on. We were given the exciting task of selling Chuck Wagon Candy Patties. Yeah, right, I had enough problems trying to raise money for food to eat.

Teachers were milling around, organizing the students with their perspective boxes of chocolates and sending them on their way. Students were squealing with excitement about the upcoming activity.

As I sat in the gymnasium feeling gloomy, the idea came to me like a freight train smashing into a brick wall. *What if I took some of the bars and sold them in place of the corsages? Surely, they would be easier to sell! Who doesn't love chocolate?* The plan was perfect! I felt guilty about the idea of taking these bars, yet the thought of another beating from my brutish brother pushed me into the arms of thievery.

Thievery's embrace was sweet as she shielded me from the stone fists that threatened to harm me each day. When there seemed to be not a soul to witness my steal-away, I grabbed a box of chocolates and made my way toward the exit.

Using my mother as my unsuspecting getaway driver, we fled the school grounds with my booty. This day changed my life and the small world I lived in. I lived in a world filled with fear and disappointments, hunger, and uncertainties. Helplessness surrounded me. I was a victim of my circumstance.

There seemed no escape, but I could hold this one victory close and never let it go. I wanted to help my mother in her pursuit of stability. This day changed my life. This day I became a contributor of sorts. This day paved the way for many more days of taking from the rich and giving to the poor. My Robin Hood days had arrived.

The following day I returned to school and made a second run at stealing the candy bars for my own gain. Anxiously, I climbed into my mother's car, victorious.

After this, I began stealing from stores, taking candy bars, grabbing teddy bears, anything I could get my sticky fingers on. Desperation pushed me further each time.

As I retrieved the items, my sister would hold the door open to make my escape easier. When our treasures were picked and my hands were full, I would sneak past the cashiers and make a run for it with my sister at my flank. Once safely in the car with our getaway driver, played by my mother, we would speed off disappearing into the congested streets. The people were buzzing about on their own missions, the business of completing their daily tasks.

Once far enough away from the scene of the crime and comfortable on our own turf, we would sell the bars of candy and miscellaneous items that once belonged to the store we had just fled. We were selling the candy for five dollars a box as I was sure to take the pricy gourmet sorts, chocolate Millionaires among others.

This was certainly an upgrade from the fifty-cent flowers. Once we sold our booty, we would turn over the money to our mother. I felt like a necessary provider for our much-needed funds. I had arrived. I was a thief, a schemer, and a pint-sized criminal. I felt as though we were rolling in the dough. In comparison to where we were, my life of thievery made things a bit easier.

For a time, things seemed to get a smidgen better. I truly felt as though I were Robin Hood, robbing the rich and giving to the poor. My siblings were my Merry Men and sidekicks. We were so successful; in fact, it gave us the confidence to begin going into office buildings to sell. We would sell our goods while searching for other opportunities.

On more than one occasion, we would take from the purses of the employees that had abandoned their desks briefly for a quick bathroom break. We would ransack the purses and take any money found. This newfound confidence resulted in my upgrading to department stores and making out with jewelry and clothes. I was bold. I was determined.

I would strut directly back into the same store to give them my speech. "I bought these clothes for my mom, only they don't fit. She wants me to return them, but I can't find my receipt." I was good. I dared anyone to put me to the test. Each time the salesclerk would readily give the money to me for the items. I knew how to work them.

I was only in fifth grade around this time and becoming quite the con artist. I would provide the cashiers with fake addresses and names. There were many more scenarios to follow.

Convenience stores became an easy way to get our hands on a few bucks. My sister would distract the cashier, and I would simply take the money bag from underneath the counter! Most workers never suspected us to do such a thing as I was a young girl. In part, this is what made it so successful. My mom, ever the faithful getaway driver, would be perched outside, awaiting our return. Mom would rip up any checks and flush them down the toilet when we arrived home.

If we needed a lawnmower or if I wanted a bicycle, I stole it. I took from the upscale stores and gifted myself and my poor Merry Men with the goods.

I didn't want my family going hungry, so I began stealing food. My sister and I went into supermarkets. She covered my back, and I carried an empty brown paper bag and filled it with anything I thought looked appealing. My mother instructed us to stick to our prerehearsed story if ever we were caught. She warned us not to waver. If we did, we would be thrown in jail.

Our reaction to being caught was a key factor in our storytelling. We must look shocked and completely innocent. We lied about our ages, always younger than we actually were. Our clothes, of course, told a tale within themselves as we were always poorly dressed. Sniffling, we told our accusers that we had been sent to the store by our parents, but had left our money at home or lost it on the way. As innocent children, we knew no better than to take our "ill-gotten gain" back to our home. We were certain that our parents would repay the debt once they learned the store had not been paid.

We would get caught from time to time but were released from questioning and deemed innocent as our story never changed. I was fearless and scared of nothing. My sister, Adelia, and I also made quite the team of bandits. Most of our quality time was spent practicing hunting and gathering.

We were like well-trained soldiers on a reconnaissance mission as we sought out the stores that looked to be the best options. Once in, I would gather the booty. Much like the Native Americans I recalled hearing about in school, the goal in mind was always the same: food and shelter. Was it so wrong after all? These were the well-to-do, and we were the starving poor, unable to find other means of survival.

Things were moving along well, and we got better as time wore on. Soon my conscience was seared, and our heists no longer seemed to be wrong, immoral, or unlawful. I just factored it into my daily activities, like a job or a chore. I began to lose sight of right and wrong altogether.

This made my life less complicated, and I began going through the motions, like a robot doing what had to be done. Until one day on one of our thieving adventures, I stole a money bag and stuffed it in my pants. Upon our hasty return home, I discovered a loaded gun within its contents. It occurred to me then that the gun could have been used on me or my sister while in the process of robbing the store.

It shook me up enough to discourage me from wanting to continue. I had never considered what we did as being dangerous and rarely had there been any negative repercussions for stealing. This changed things for me. I washed my hands of it all and refused to continue. Needless to say, my stepfather was not happy with this decision.

To encourage me to continue, he locked me in my dingy room. For days I went without food or water. I was locked away like a prisoner. In those moments and many like them, I often wondered if it would be easier for me to just die. My only peace was that my stepfather had stopped making an appearance at the foot of my bed, at least for the time being.

Every morning I would wake again to the real nightmare—the one I was living in. Locked in my room for days, I became weak with hunger. This proved to be effective as I found myself once again ransacking purses and taking from the rich to give to the poor. I assured myself, I needed to eat, didn't I?

Shortly thereafter, I was caught in the act of stealing. My short stay locked in my room seemed but a dream as

I was now thrown into jail. At this stage I was in seventh grade. I never expected to land in jail. Robin Hood never got caught! I knew what I was doing had been wrong, yet I didn't see that I had a choice. When those cold hand cuffs were digging into my wrists, I thought their impressions would last a lifetime. This memory surely would. Racing thoughts littered my mind, making it difficult to think straight.

Sitting in the back of a patrol car, I felt all the many spinning plates I had learned to balance so well came crashing down around me. I could envision myself in a small boat spinning out of control, hitting every rock and boulder along the way. I was at the edge of a waterfall. In my descent I began taking on water, filling my lungs and striking me down with terror.

Upon arrival at the police station, I was passed through different stages of the booking process. The police officers seemed to me to be very harsh, unkind, and looking at me with disgust. I felt I was just another piece of trash that needed to be locked away or thrown out with the garbage. At the time, I was an unruly kid. I had no compassion for these men and the duties they were performing. Looking back, I realized the officers were protecting the community and putting their lives on the line each day.

As the interrogations continued, the florescent lights burned my already stinging eyes. Their soft buzzing noise kept ringing in my ears. The officers continued barking demands at me with ominous instructions to follow. Their demeanor and language left me with threatening hints hanging in the air.

There were no windows, only long white glossy walls and hallways as far as the eye could see. Loud buzzers would go off periodically, announcing the comings and goings of the officers leaving one room to enter another.

Everything was monitored. I noticed cameras scattered about in the room where I stood. I was instructed to stand behind a yellow piece of tape on the floor while they asked me questions and did what looked to be heaps of paperwork. I couldn't imagine why. I had stolen. They caught me. End of story.

I waited there for what seemed forever before they escorted me down a long white hallway winding toward our destination, where I was surely to be disappointed with the accommodations. The cold air surrounded me as the hall stretched on. This was not what I had expected to have happen. It never occurred to me that I might actually get caught. Where were my Merry Men when I needed them?

I put one foot in front of the other. I focused on the movement of my feet in order to hold myself together, and as always I held my tears at bay. I had become good at it by this point and showed little sign of emotion. In my world, there was no room for self-pity. It only got in the way of doing what had to be done and enduring the rest.

I wondered if this was to be my future but was told nothing regarding how long my stay would be. I sat for hours contemplating the implications after I was deposited in a small white stone-covered cell. This surely was not the Ritz-Carlton. My thoughts were like Dorothy in the Wizard of Oz: "Toto, we're not in Kansas anymore." The air gave me a chill, and the blanket given to me by a heavyset woman with a raspy voice was full of holes. It provided little warmth or shielding from the ever-glowing lights that were never turned off.

As I sat in silence, a tiny whisper brushed past my lips. A hint of gratitude and peace rested softly on my shoulders. Like a feather, it slid through the air calming my mind. My one consolation was I was safe. No one could hurt me in that place of solitude. I was blanketed in safety, if only for a little while.

This became my home for the next week. It seemed to be a great deal longer stay than that. There was scarcely anything to do. The police officers would wake us up every morning at 5:00 a.m. to run laps in the courtyard until we were weak and on the verge of throwing up the contents of our dinner from the night before. Following this, we would clean and mop the same cement floors we had mopped the morning before.

After our early morning duties, we were served whatever assortment of scraps they had left over in the kitchen from the previous day, prepared by other inmates. I kept my head down most of the time, not knowing what to expect from my fellow lawbreakers. My only friends were the crickets that serenaded me to sleep at the end of each day.

I felt alone and was gripped more than once by the fear of never being released. But each night as I lay down and my eye lids grew heavy with exhaustion. I knew that this night I could rest easy knowing that my stepfather couldn't penetrate these jail walls. Hallelujah!

In spite of this, I would often cry out in my sleep. I would wake up in a cold sweat for I couldn't escape the hands of my stepfather even in my dreams. I found that it mattered little where I fell asleep. The nightmares were still the same.

A week later, I was released and was forced back into reality. I had survived. When I returned home, I received no comfort from my parents whatsoever. They assured me that it was my carelessness that had gotten me thrown into jail.

When I returned to school, I often schemed of ways to alert my teachers as to what I was up to in hopes there would be something they could do to help. No one seemed to want to get involved for fear of the implications. They had a healthy fear of the Jones family. Admittedly, we were terrible, and I could understand their apprehension. I could appreciate any attempt to speak out would be to no avail. So once more I felt helpless.

I had no direction and was struggling to keep my grades at a passing level. The emptiness I felt inside often made me wonder if there was something more to life. How could there not be more than this? I had no exposure to the idea of God and had heard very little throughout my life on the topic.

I was not brought up in a Christian home. Therefore, we did not attend church, read the Bible, or pray. Jesus, who was Jesus? He was as far away as the Milky Way, so I thought. The golden rule in most homes was, "Do unto others as you would have them do unto you." My rule was to do unto others before they had a chance to do unto you.

Although my family did not go to church, my siblings and I would make our appearance occasionally. A church bus began making trips to our less fortunate part of town to pick up people to go to church. The bus dropped us off at this small, quaint church known as the Davis Boulevard Baptist church. My stepfather did not approve of this and many times forbade us from going. If he were drinking that day, which was most of the time, you could just forget about going to church.

My stepfather began calling me a Jesus freak. His abusive nature had no bounds and held no respect for this so-called Jesus. From his prospective, it was a waste of an hour. He thought it was ridiculous for us to go. Therefore, our trips to this small safe-haven of peace were few and far between. In the beginning of our Sunday trips, it was just a means to get out of the house for a couple of hours. A seed, however small, had been planted in my mind. Deep down I knew there was something more to life. I wanted to know more.

Sadly, my desire to pursue this further was of no use when it came to my stepfather. It was clear he was unhappy. It angered him to see joy of any shade in our lives. He would quickly pour his black shade of paint over our existence to blot out its beauty. I soon gave up hope for this Jesus person. I didn't think he would be interested in helping someone like me. Instead, I continued down the path of stealing from the rich and giving to the poor just like Robin Hood and his Merry Men.

My Sister and I in a Smoke Filled Honky Tonk
Selling Homemade Toilet Paper Flowers

CHAPTER 3

SCHOOL-DAY PRANKS

My feelings of hopeless and despair were affecting every facet of my life. In school I channeled my emotions with anger and rebellion. This was no secret, and often I found myself in physical altercations with other students, many times with boys, but I was tough and won more times than not. I was a poor student, not because I was lacking in intellect but simply because my mother was often taking us out of school to make money. I lacked the discipline and the study skills required for success. Because of this, I was put into special education classes. This turned out to be something of a blessing as my special education teacher, Mrs. Moore, chose to take me under her wing.

I can still recall her face because she was so kind to me, something that I was certainly not used to. She had no self-serving agenda in doing so, which was hard for me to wrap my mind around. This was a foreign concept in my world. She was like an angel sent to me from this elusive Jesus to help me along to the next stepping-stone of life.

Things began to look up academically shortly after my joining Mrs. Moore's class. My self-esteem began to peek out from beneath the covers. I began to build a sense of pride and began to take my studies more seriously. I blossomed under the watchful and caring eyes of my beloved teacher.

I was still very troubled and deeply unhappy, so it came as no surprise to anyone, including myself, that disaster struck yet again. I became unruly, destructive, and my bad behavior was more and more frequent.

I wanted so badly to be accepted and be a part of the crowd. I started to pull all kinds of stunts in my attempt to seek approval and recognition. My upbringing brought out the violent side of me, and I started acting out, like a mad dog. All a person had to do was say, "Sick 'em," and I was ready to attack like a rabid animal.

One day we were out in the school yard with our PE teacher, Mr. Sighcheck. He gave me instructions on a physical activity I did not want to do. I said, "No!"

Needless to say, he did not like my answer. With a stern look in his eyes, he started toward me. He repeated his command, and again I said, "No."

His response was, "Okay, young lady, you are going to the principal's office."

I replied, "No, I am not going!"

He reminded me of a charging bull as he rushed toward me. His face turned beet red, his nostrils began to flare out, and with each step he was snarling and grumbling under his breath. He reached out to grab me, and like a speeding bullet I shot off running. I was running faster than an African cheetah.

The race was on, and all the kids in the school yard were cheering me on. "Go, Jones! Go, Jones! Go, Jones! Go!" The screams and laughter made me feel like I was a gold medal athlete at the Olympics.

I had youth on my side, and to his dismay, Mr. Sighcheck would never have been able to catch me. The bell rang, and I stopped running and fell to the ground. Mr. Sighcheck, out of breath and struggling to talk, reached out his hand to grab me. Like a pro-football player, I thrust my leg upward and soundly kicked him right between the legs. He doubled over in pain and fell to the ground.

When he was finally able to catch his breath, he stood up, and I found myself being dragged down the hallway on the way to the principal's office. Another teacher, Mrs. Bryan, was witnessing the scene. I was not going quietly. I was grappling, kicking, and screaming. It took two teachers to wrestle down this unruly child.

None of the kids in the school liked Mrs. Bryan because she was so mean to everyone. She came across like a sergeant in the military. Some kids called her the Gestapo. She gave me that "Go to you-know-where" look, and it wasn't heaven. Her eyes were fiery red, and with a hateful tone she said to my PE instructor, "Why don't you just pick her up and carry her to the office." She was so angry because I refused to walk.

This period of time I was in grade school, and I got expelled. My age did not matter. What kid gets expelled from grade school!

On another occasion, my classmates and I were in the hallway, waiting to get into the cafeteria lunch line. I was standing behind a teacher by the name of Mrs. Haas. The boy behind me whispered in my ear, "I dare you to pop the teacher's bra strap."

My mind whirled, "Why didn't I think of that? It would be really funny, and I might win some brownie points with the kids." After all, I was Robin Hood, a very mischievous character. So I pulled out my imaginary bow and arrow, my hand being the bow and the teacher's delicate undergarment my arrow. I pulled back on Mrs. Haas bra strap and *pop*! I had hit the mark, which echoed a resounding noise down the hallway.

I was elated as I heard an outcry of uncontrollable laughter coming from all the students. Of course, my delight turned into disappointment when I was once again marched off to the principal's office. Even though I was being scolded and reprimanded for my outrageous behavior, I could not help but take joy in the fact that I had made the entire student body laugh at my antics.

At the time, I thought my bratty conduct was funny, even hilarious. I will never forget a girl in my class by the name of Daisy, a real bully. Daisy reveled in making misery for the other children. I watched this bully pick on the innocent, and yet she was a coward, a spineless worm.

One day in school she flipped me off, and I did not like that. Naturally, I wanted revenge! I knew I would get back at her somehow.

Walking to school each day, I passed by a small creek. I suddenly came up with a bright idea, a brilliant plan. I walked to the creek and began to scrounge around for a "crawdaddy"—at least in my little world that is what we called them. Some people call them crawdads or crawfish. For those of you who have not had the pleasure of dining on this Southern delicacy, they look like miniature lobsters with pincher claws and bugged-out eyes. After a while, I finally captured one of the little creatures and took him to school with me.

Like a thief in the night, I managed to deposit my crawdaddy in Daisy's lunch sack. I slipped out of sight with a sweet, innocent look on my face. I thought lunchtime would never arrive. I had taken into confidence two of my classmates, my Merry Men. Together we went into the lunch room with an air of excitement about us.

We sat down, our eyes glued on Daisy. We surely did not want to miss the show of the century. I will never forget the look of horror on her face as she reached into her lunch sack and came out with a crawdaddy attached to her hand. Her scream was so loud it drowned out all the other noises in the lunchroom. Daisy threw the crawdaddy up in the air. It went one way, and she went another. Mayhem filled the room. The kids were rolled over in hysterical laughter, the teachers were scurrying about trying to determine what was causing all the hubbub, the cafeteria workers had grabbed brooms and mops, and I gloated as my revenge was complete.

The next sound I remember hearing came across the school's intercom system. "Jeanette Jones, please report to the principal's office." I can't imagine why the staff assumed I was the villainous prankster. Nevertheless, I marched into the office with my head held high.

I received the same lecture as I always did. I was very disappointed that my Merry Men and I had to come up with a grand total of thirty-five cents to buy Daisy's lunch. I guess she didn't like crawdaddys.

Trips to the principal's office typically ended with the usual scolding and reprimands. As my escapades began to escalate, I found myself in the middle of an altercation with a peer and got expelled from school. This, however, was not the first time I had been expelled. By the seventh grade, I was expelled from Birdville ISD for setting a jukebox on fire. The stench of the plastic melting into a tar-like substance was overpowering as I watched it crackle and pop.

I don't know why I did it to this day. Bystanders suspected I didn't like the music, but realistically, I just wanted to watch it burn. It seemed much like my life, crumbling into a pile of ashes and blown away by the wind. I was destined to live each day like the last. School days, school days, turned into Jeanette Jones's unruly school days!

CHAPTER 4

SWIMMING UPRIVER

Many times over the years, I felt as though my siblings and I were swimming upriver. It was much like the salmon swimming against the current of torrent waters in an effort to get to their destination. My siblings chose to go one way, and I went another. In the end, it was me and me alone who made the precarious journey struggling my way upstream. My efforts paid off as I came to the end of my quest. Unlike my siblings, I was not overtaken by the violent waters of the turbulent river. The strength I drew from was the desire to please my mother and earn her love. That desire pushed me inch by inch further and further up the river.

At a very young age, it was clear I was set apart from my siblings. We had very different ways of handling the painful realities to which we were all victims. The heavy drug usage, drunkenness, and varied unlawful activities were a source of intense stabbing pains that would torment any sane person. My siblings were drawn to what the world could offer to quiet their minds and numb their physical and mental torture. They succumbed to the use of drugs and alcohol, which slowly but surely left its mark, corroding their decaying lives. It became impossible for them to blot out the painful truths and horrible realities of their existence. They couldn't escape the grips of addictions.

I have limited memories of my two older brothers, Alfred Jones, age 15, and Harrison Jones, age 16. They left home when I was very young. However, my other brothers, Chase and Brett, were very present in my life. Many nights these boys would head out to their perspective hole-in-the-wall honky-tonks. In the English language, *honky-tonks* can be translated as low-budget forms of entertainment. Most nights my brothers would wind up in bar brawls. My brother Brett would inevitably return home proudly with a bar prize. I called these bar trinkets whores, yet he could care less about their station in life. His only care was the pleasures they would offer him. They would barge in like a circus coming to town around two o'clock in the morning and busy themselves in a way that was sure to wake me up.

My other brother Chase would at times return home from his honky-tonk escapades, and if he had been unsuccessful in bringing home his door prize for the night, he would storm into my room. In his drunken stupor, he would get his thrills by taking a turn with me. The lack of sleep made it challenging for me to focus in school most days.

My sisters, Adelia and Grace, also kicked up their heels with their fair share of excitement. They, too, found it challenging to stay out of trouble. I recall on one occasion stumbling over my sister's limp body on the garage floor. She had at some point passed out from sniffing gasoline in an effort to get high or commit suicide. I was never certain which one of the two was her final intention. My mother had 911 on speed dial at this chapter of our lives. The EMTs arrived almost as quickly as the number was dialed. Knowing exactly where we lived, there was no need for them to waste their time getting directions to our all-too-familiar address. Our house must have seemed like a second home to them. Many of them knew us by name because of the frequency in which they were called. This turned out to be a weekly basis, which was an alarmingly high occasion.

There were few similarities in myself and my siblings. I never considered abusing drugs or drowning my grief in alcohol. In many ways, it seemed to only amplify their pain. It would be like taking a knife to an already bleeding wound. It was difficult to watch the lives of my siblings, my blood kin, simply unravel at my feet. They were drifting slowly from my reach, leaving me even more alone in this dark place. I began to search for other outlets.

The only thing that I did want, in fact, was a place I could call home. I wanted a normal life. I wanted the love of my mother, which I pursued with vigor to no avail. This void in my life caused me to seek out some other source of happiness. I found an outlet in sports. I played basketball, volleyball, and ran track. Basketball in the end won my heart. I was athletically gifted, and this proved to be a good tool for me to channel my pain and frustrations. I enjoyed the time away from home, time I could forget about the terror I was living in and find some comfort and peace of mind if even for just a few hours.

My athleticism was not enough to snuff out the stigma that came with being a Jones. My peers were sure to slander me with their venomous words. My clothes were from Goodwill, and theirs were bought new with name-brand tags. They snubbed their noses at me as I did not fit in. Despite their hateful sneers, I was determined to prove myself, to show my fellow students that you did not have to have money to achieve your goals. I used my athletic ability as an effort to gain acceptance.

My stepfather did not like the joy sports brought to me and would interfere as often as he could. Many times, he would attempt to prevent me from attending the games. On one occasion he and all his 6'4", 245-pound self stomped right onto the court midgame and dragged me out by my hair in front of the onlookers. I could hear the gasps and murmurs all around me, yet nobody wanted to stand up to a devil out of fear of retaliation. This dramatic and brutal display by my stepfather was surely etched in the minds of all who witnessed it. It did not, of course, aid in my efforts to realign the outlook of my peers toward me.

My school days were lonely, and I had little to no friends until I met Carrie Chapman. Carrie did not judge me by my last name and tattered clothes. We became fast friends and did most things together. We decided to try out for cheerleading. I knew I had a fair shot at making the team. I was able to do many of the jumps and stunts of the more seasoned cheerleaders. I could do high jumps, splits and round off toe touches. Because I was tiny. I did not have much body weight to lift off the ground. Carrie did not embody these skills; however, she was beautiful, and beautiful girls were always readily accepted. There was always room for them. One thing in my favor was that the judges were from out of town. Fortunately for me, there were no student body voters.

The days to follow were filled with making posters to amplify the excitement surrounding the votes. The students took a piece of cloth, decorated it and signed it for good luck. My sister Adelia was so kind to write me a little note that read, "Violets are blue, and shit reminds me of you." Adelia did not mean to be vulgar in her attempt to support me. This was simply a way of life for our family. This was normal language for us. I proudly pinned this on my shirt for the day. Not the most encouraging or appropriate saying, yet not one teacher said a word about it. Again, my last name itself was enough to send a tremor through anyone. I still have that ribbon from Adelia with the number 5 at the top. Little did I know she would die at a young age, and this was the only thing that I have now to remember her by.

When the day finally came to reveal the big winners, I recall how anxious I felt. We tried out at 9:00 a.m. that morning. We did not get called back to the auditorium until 3:00 p.m. that afternoon. This was the big day, the day they would be announcing the cheerleaders for the 1975–1976 school year. I still remember them calling my name, "Jeanette Jones, first cheerleader." I stood there stunned before running up to the stage to take my place and wait for my best friend to join me. Sadly, much to my surprise, Carrie did not make the team. This was difficult for me to accept, yet I was excited to accept the challenge and become a part of the ninth grade cheerleading squad.

Standing in the principal's office, I rang home hoping to catch my mother on the line. Instead I got the devil, my stepfather. My emotions were naturally stirred. Before I could think, excitedly I proclaimed, "I made the squad!" Instead of congratulations, my stepfather informed me that he was praying that I wouldn't make the team. I was witty and had the mouth of a sailor, compliments of my family. I belligerently sounded off. "I didn't know you knew how to pray!" I then continued to say things that require too much editing to list here. He didn't care for that, as you can imagine. Spitefully, he told me I had two choices: I could move out or quit the team.

Given the fact that I was not staying at a resort-style spa in my house of torture, this was not a difficult decision to make. I would move out. I would be fine. Unfortunately, at the young age of fourteen, it proved challenging to find a place to live and a means to support myself. I fell once more into despair, feeling trapped with the prospect of being forced to quit the team I had worked so hard to join. It was during this time that I made a choice in the depths of my despair to end my life. Let's just say I was gun shy, so I decided to take a different route to accomplish my goal. It didn't take me long to get hold of a bottle of pills, which I thought must have been lethal. I had on many occasions seen my sister taking such pills to get high.

I did not want to get high. I just wanted to die. Shortly after attaining the narcotics, I took the entire bottle and waited. At some point, everything became convoluted and foggy. I lost consciousness. It was during this time of my unconscious drugged-up state that something quite unexpected and miraculous happened to me. I saw God as if in a cloud. He began to speak to me. The words He whispered to me were profound. He let me know through this visitation that He had plans for my life. Little did I know how big His plans for me were going to become. I do recall His presence and the peace and love that wrapped around me like an embrace. I knew little of God. However, when I finally came to after throwing up the poisons and expelling the death I thought would befall me, I reflected on my experience. I would not realize the full impact my encounter with God was to have on my life in years to come.

After my short recovery from this failed suicide attempt, I decided that with or without a plan, I was leaving. My sister happened upon me in the midst of my preparations and decided that she too would leave. We packed a few things quietly in order to alert no one of our departure. We left like a thief in the night—in fact, we had truly earned the title "thief." We walked along, side by side up to a certain point. My sister went one way and I another. I made my way on foot to Carrie's house. I knew her parents were kind people and would let me stay a night, maybe more. Carrie's folks welcomed me with open arms. I began to tell them some of the things that had been going on-well, a PG 13 version anyway. They were horrified and immediately insisted that I stay for the night.

That same night, there came a knock at the door. The devil had come to pay these nice people a visit. They hid me well and fabricated a story, insisting that I was not at their home. My stepfather did not believe them and said as much. He left to return home and sent the cops by to search the grounds, as he was certain I was hiding there. We only had a window of time to revise our plan before the police arrived. Carrie's folks decided to take me to another relative's house, where I slept that evening. I returned to school the next morning. That afternoon I was called to the principal's office. They informed me that my parents were there and wanted to speak with me. I reported to the office. When I came into the room, a chill filled the air, and I felt I was swimming in cold waters, surrounded by icebergs. I stood firm my ground because I knew my parents' intent was to take me with them. Boldly, I curtly blurted out the words, "I am most certainly not going back with you and to the hellhole you call home."

I walked away bravely and fled the school property. I headed back to Carrie's house. My stay there was short as Child Welfare came knocking. They informed the Chapmans and me that I could not live with someone outside of my family. To avoid returning home, I reached out to my brother Brett and went to stay with him and his wife. This, too, was short-lived given the fact that he began sexually assaulting me despite being a married man. He did not seem to care. This was happening on a regular basis after school. I made the choice to leave and make my way to the next couch I was to sleep on.

One of my sisters, Adelia, was now living with a man who had recently been released from prison for murder. I knew also that he was abusive and had recently knocked some of my sister's teeth out during a rage. As difficult a decision this was for me to make, I decided not to be his next punching bag and fled to my other sister Grace's place. Grace had recently lost her husband, Ethan, to cancer. She was not in good spirits and had a very dysfunctional home. In spite of her young daughter's presence, Grace ran wild in her pursuits to find love to dull the pain of her sudden loss. She would go out and come home late in the evenings with strange men. Many times, I would be awakened on the couch only to feel the weight of a strange man on top of me attempting to sexually abuse me. I would fight them off with all the strength I had in me. Finally, I grew weary of this and fled to the streets. It was not from fear. I was not afraid. I knew I could take care of myself. I fled out of a burning desire for peace. I desired to be rid of that world and all the disgusting creatures it brought with it. They were like demons trying to claw their way right through to my soul. I knew I had no choice but to live on the streets. I was out of places to go, and I did not have a road map.

The road map of life is more important than any other. As an adolescent, I never thought about the road of life or the path that I would follow. As I grew into a young adult, I learned the difficulty of traveling life's path without a map. What I eventually came to understand is that life is like following an unfamiliar path. You cannot predict where it will take you. Thinking you are on the right highway, you move toward the direction it leads from one destination to another and quickly learn it is not always a straight thoroughfare.

At the beginning of my quest, I knew I would encounter curves and sharp crooked turns. Understanding that I may have to cross rugged old bridges without side rails, I journeyed forward. Fearlessly, I traveled down the side of a mountain without being able to see the bottom. There were dark tunnels, wet and slick pathways, detours, obstacles, and roadblocks along the way. Yet I continued with my conquest of searching for a better life.

I learned early in life if you take a road trip and go on a route that you have not driven before, you will probably be stopping and asking for directions. When I started down this one particular road, I never dreamed where it would lead me or take me! At the time my thoughts were, *Wherever the road takes me is better than where I am now.*

I threw a few of my tattered and faded clothes into a small bag and walked away without looking back. After all, there was nothing to look back to. I just had to look forward.

I began my road trip, and with each new day I hitchhiked, walked, hitchhiked and walked. I was physically strong and fit because I was very athletic. I loved many sports, and I still do. After walking for so long, my legs began to shake like jelly. *I must find a resting place*, I thought.

Struggling to go on, I saw a bridge in the near distance. I forced myself to get to that bridge. As I approached it, it felt like an old familiar friend as it drew me in. I drove my imaginary car under the bridge and parked it. Finally! I had found a place to find refuge and safety. For now, I was in my own world, the only one in control. The chaos that had been ruling my life seemed to momentarily subside.

I sat solemnly as my eyes took in my surroundings. My new home did not look as regal as the Taj Mahal in India, nor the palace in Versailles, France, yet its lack of beauty and decorum could not be compared to its grand purpose.

As dusk began to hover over, two small cottontail rabbits appeared out of nowhere. They played leapfrog over each other. When they got tired of that game, they started running back and forth as if they were in a NASCAR race. It was very calming watching the two small creatures play without a care in the world. I wondered, *Why couldn't I have been a rabbit?*

The sun began to drop slowly, and before long darkness covered me like a blanket. The sounds of night began to come alive. Crickets started chirping, frogs started croaking, and occasionally, I could hear the hoot of an owl. I think they were all in a church choir singing just for me.

I made a pillow out of the few clothes I had stuffed in a bag. I lay my head down from sheer exhaustion and extreme physical and mental fatigue.

There was a steady sound of cars as their tires clicked over the bridge. I wondered, *Where could all these people be going? Were they lost? Perhaps they didn't have a road map*. I couldn't answer my own questions. My body was aching from the miles of walking and the stress of hitchhiking. I fell asleep not by counting sheep but counting tire clicks.

My day would begin at five o'clock each morning. I would hitchhike to school each day. It was thirty miles one way. On Saturday mornings I had cheerleading practice. Try as I did, I was unable to make it on occasions. The head cheerleader, Rita Whirley, informed me that if I were to miss anymore, she would kick me off the team. Cheerleading, at that time, I thought was all I had left. I was not going to allow myself to miss another practice.

I would practice barefoot, given that I only had one pair of shoes and did not want to mess them up. This was humiliating but nothing out of the ordinary. I was the black sheep of my squad, so what difference did it make if I practiced barefooted? They all knew I had no money to pay for cheerleading.

On one Saturday morning, I stepped on a piece of glass on my way to practice and cut a gash in my foot. I did not let this stop me in my pursuit to make practice. I did not want to be kicked off of the team, so I continued hobbling down the side of the road. A man, whom I now believe was an angel sent from God Himself, offered me a ride. I took it and arrived safely and on time to practice that morning. This was the first time I had been alone with a man who did not abuse me.

With glass in foot, I arrived at Lori's house for practice. My foot was bleeding, and I could smell a stench coming off me that was nauseating. I had nowhere to shower or wash my clothes. I only had a few things to wear. Mrs. Kurtz and Mrs. Fletcher took one look at me, and they could tell I was in a bad way. They also saw my wounded foot and insisted on removing the piece of glass, cleaning and dressing the wound. They informed me that there would be a pool party after practice and they would like me to stay to join in. I am certain they felt sorry for me.

I knew this would be a bad idea, given I had no bathing suit, and certainly did not want to be caught hitchhiking late at night. However, they insisted I stay and provided me with a bathing suit. Against my better judgment, I stayed. They had a big Laguna-like pool with a tall slide attached. I made my way to the top of the slide. Before I was securely seated, I lost my balance and fell from the slide. I injured my left foot and sliced my left ankle wide open. Blood began to stream from my leg. Alarmed, Mrs. Kurtz asked me how she could get in touch with my parents.

I, of course, did not want tell her about my parents. I told her that my mother had moved to California, abandoning her family. I was literally living on the streets, but did not want Mrs. Kurtz to know this. She insisted that I was badly injured and needed medical attention. I told her to take me to the John Peter Smith Hospital. I didn't know much about this hospital, but what I did know is that any time anyone in my family got injured, that is where they went. This state-owned hospital, I assumed, was a low-budget facility where individuals without insurance would go.

Mrs. Kurtz took me to the hospital. The emergency room staff stitched up my wounds and informed me that I was one of the luckiest girls in the world. I had nearly severed my Achilles tendon. Had this happened, I would have spent the rest of my life dragging my foot behind me. Mrs. Kurtz and her daughter, who was also on my squad, took me home with them that night. Her daughter, Terri, was as kind as her mother and always treated me with respect. With their growing concern for my circumstances, Mrs. Kurtz allowed me to sleep in her home for the night. This was the first night in a while that I did not have to sleep outside on the streets.

Mrs. Kurtz worked for Fort Worth congressman Jim Wright, Speaker of the United States House of Representatives. With his assistance, she began her homework. She ran due diligence reports on my family. She ran background checks and pulled criminal histories. She knew something was terribly wrong and realized I needed help. She allowed me to continue staying at their home. She began a file to keep all her findings of the Jones family. She had a hunch that one day it may prove useful to have such information.

The Kurtz family was warm, kind, and loving. I had never seen a home like this. Her husband, Richard, was the first man I grew to trust, and to follow was her son, Kevin. They took me in and never treated me like a nuisance. They went to church on Sundays and spoke of God's grace and love very often. I had never felt such peace and love. The thought of being taken from this place was heart wrenching, but I knew the time would come. Or so I thought. It was as if I fell asleep and was in a dream. I would study their interactions closely to try to understand the way they embraced and smiled warmly at one another.

This precious family also supplied me with new clothes, shoes, coats, and whatever else I needed. They treated me like a daughter. Things were coming along well. But of course, dead dogs won't lie. My stepfather continued to call Child Services and cause trouble. They finally forced me to stay with my aunt Betty, my stepfather's sister. This is where I became Cinderella. I was used to be her maid servant. "Cinderella, get me this! Cinderella, get me that! Cinderella, mop the floors, clean the toilets, cook the meals, wash the dishes!" She threw whatever dirty chore she could at me.

Aunt Betty spent most of her time cheating on her husband, which did not leave her with adequate time to clean the house. Imagine that! She was constantly ordering me to clean this or that, and then she would deem it unsatisfactory and make me start over. I would be grounded for playing with my four nephews. Aunt Betty didn't want me to enjoy life at all. She had the same attitude as her brother, my stepfather. They were dysfunctional in their own way, like the rest of my family. During this time, I would question myself yet again and wonder if there were any decent human beings in this world? The Kurtz family not included, of course.

The mornings before school became my only solace as the Kurtz family would pick me up and take me to school. They would allow me to stay with them as much as was possible. They were very much aware of my growing unhappiness and my circumstances.

Days turned into weeks and weeks into months. The time I spent with the Kurtzes began to have a strong effect on me. I grew closer to them than I thought was ever possible. I continued to watch them closely. I grew more and more curious about a family that was filled with such love and peace. They were so drastically different from what I had ever experienced before. I began to wonder what it was that set them apart. What made them treat one another in such a loving manner?

The day finally came when I asked Mrs. Kurtz, "Why is it that your family is so different than anything I've ever known? I don't understand how you, day in and day out, treat one another in the loving way that you do." This is where my journey took a turn I had not foreseen or expected. Mrs. Kurtz sat me down and began sharing the message of Jesus Christ with me. She began to explain to me the message of salvation and all about this Jesus person. I sat very still as I soaked up every single word she said like a sponge. Oh, how I wanted to be a part of anything that offered this type of love, peace, grace, and unending mercy.

As she spoke, I began to have more and more questions build up inside me. I remember thinking, *Well, it's easy for you to embrace the love of this Jesus. You are not dirty like I am. I certainly am not worthy to be a part of such grace and forgiveness.*

I asked Mrs. Kurtz many questions and laid before her my doubts, concerns, and reservations. I told her how I felt like spoiled goods, too rotten and dirty to be loved or forgiven. I felt as though maybe I should wait a few years and clean up my life. It would be then and only then would I dare to feel worthy and clean enough to approach her Jesus with my proposition of becoming a part of the "club," as I saw it.

Mrs. Kurtz was very patient and listened to my concerns and doubts. With a smile on her face, she taught me a truth that forever changed my existence and life forever. She shared with me about the free gift of eternal life as opposed to the death I thought was surely due me. She taught me about the gift of salvation and how it could free me from all bondage. She explained how Satan had kept me bound up to prevent me from hearing the truth. Mrs. Kurtz told me about the sacrifice that Jesus made to blot our sins. She explained how He was sent to walk among us, carrying the message of grace, and how He died on the cross to forgive our ever-growing and never-ending sins. She told me He did this so we could be with Him in this life and the life to follow.

She explained that I didn't need to clean my life up first, but to come as I was. She said, "Jesus died for the sinner. He will always leave His flock to pursue His lost sheep. He loves you where you are and will not demand you tidy up or rid yourself of your shortcomings before running into His arms."

She read from her Bible John 3:16 (King James Version):

> For God so loved the world, that he gave his only begotten Son, that whosoever believeth in him should not perish, but have everlasting life.

She also explained that all I had to do is simply understand, believe, and accept that He died for my sins and ask Him to come into my life and my heart. There was no action or chore I could do to earn or lose His love. There was nothing I could do to save myself. His death on the cross had secured my salvation.

Mrs. Kurtz read Romans 10:9–10, 13 (King James Version):

> That if thou shalt confess with thy mouth the Lord Jesus, and shalt believe in thine heart that God hath raised Him from the dead, thou shalt be saved. For with the heart man believeth unto righteousness: and with the mouth confession is made unto salvation… For whosoever shall call upon the name of the Lord shall be saved.

I remember thinking, *Wow, that is good news. Where do I sign up?*

A question-and-answer session followed before Mrs. Kurtz walked me through a salvation prayer. I asked Jesus to come into my life and to forgive all my sins. For the first time in my life, I let down my guard, and I allowed every held back emotion to burst forth. As I prayed, my eyes turned to liquid as so many tears rushed down my cheeks. A warm sensation flowed through my body as I asked for forgiveness for all my sins. As I cried out to God in repentance, it felt like the waves of the ocean were washing me clean. Jesus Christ was breaking up the hardness of my heart, washing away all my hurts, fears, and resentments. I was later baptized at First Baptist Church of North Richland Hills by Pastor Hal Brooks.

Mrs. Kurtz began to pray with me about my circumstances and for God to intervene on my behalf. I felt this to be impossible. Yet much like the salmon's survival after swimming upriver against all odds, they find themselves at their destination.

As we encounter difficult obstacles along this life's journey, it may seem we are swimming against the rushing waters. However, I am confident that we will triumph and will prove to the world that seemingly impossible goals can, in fact, be reached.

I believe that, like the salmon, we will prevail, and our success will be noticed. History will record with vigor and amazement that we overcame impossible odds.

My determination to reach this goal is as strong and deliberate as any animal's instinct to fight for survival against adverse circumstances. I realize that I have begun this difficult journey without knowing where it may lead. Neither can the salmon foresee the obstacles ahead, but he continues to pursue his course. I, too, will press onward until I reach my destination. For any who dare to take this journey that is seemingly unknown, be like the salmon and swim up the river.

CHAPTER 5

HOME SWEET HOME

I was awakened by a gentle pat and a soft voice calling my name, "Jeanette, Jeanette honey, time to get up. We don't want to be late for school." I opened my eyes to Mrs. Kurtz's warm smile.

In the distance, I could hear sounds of the hustle and bustle as each person in the house was getting ready for the day. I heard no cursing, screaming, or foul vulgar language, only friendly, kind voices could be heard in the background. The aroma of hot coffee and the smell of frying bacon filled the air. What a way to wake up. I thought I must be in heaven.

I was attending Smithfield Junior High. We drove up in front of the school, and I jumped out of the car happy as a lark. I was walking toward the school building, feeling a great sense of joy, when I heard my name being called. I came to a screeching halt when I recognized the familiar voices. As I slowly turned around, the smile left my face. I felt like someone had just hit me in the pit of my stomach. To my shock and disbelief, I saw standing there my brother Angus and my sister Adelia.

My heart did a Mexican hat dance inside my chest as I tried to act normal. Of course, I was glad to see my blood relatives, yet it brought back extremely mixed feelings of confusion and horrible memories. I stuttered and stammered as I said, "What-what, are you guys doing here?"

Angus bowed out his chest as if he were the Mafia godfather himself. He spoke to me in a stern, gruff voice, "We came after you. We're taking you back home where you belong."

I quickly replied, "No, I don't want to go back there. I like it here. This is my home."

With coldness in his eyes and sternness in his voice, he said, "This is not your home. You don't belong with these people. They're not our kind."

I sharply popped off, "Well, you can say that again!"

Angus fired back, "You'd better watch your smart mouth. I am your big brother, and it is my job to take care of you, not some other #$@&%*! strangers."

Their voices were getting louder and louder. I could see the numbers on the Richter scale going higher and higher. I knew that if this kept going, there would be a major earthquake. In order to stop the chaos, I yelled, "Okay, okay, okay! I will go with you. But first I've got to call Mrs. Kurtz. I promised her I would never leave the school without calling her."

I went to a telephone and dialed her number. First ring, no answer. Second ring, no answer. Regardless of how many times it rang, it was futile. There was no answer. I had so hoped she would answer and come save me from this situation.

I crawled into my brother's beat-up pickup. We all sat in silence, as quiet as a mouse peeing on cotton. I had lived with my family for fourteen years, and, of course, I loved them. I just didn't love the way they chose to live.

Adelia knew I was very upset, so she broke the ice, and in a cheerful voice, she said, "Guess where we're going? We're going to be staying at my boyfriend's house, Vinny. You remember him, don't you?"

I replied with my smart mouth, "Of course I remember him. He's the jerk that just got out of prison for murder! If my memory serves me correctly, isn't he the man that takes every opportunity to beat you to a pulp until you are black and blue? Oh, and let's not forget, he's the same maniac that knocked out all your beautiful white teeth. How could I ever forget him?"

At that point my brother yelled at me and said, "Shut up that smart mouth, you #$@&%*! You think you're better than anyone else? Well, you're not. You're a part of the Jones family, and you always will be. Do you hear me?"

I asked myself, *What have I done? I should not be here.*

Old memories began to flood my mind with horrific flashbacks of my life with the Jones. The last time I was with the family, they allowed my two-year old niece to smoke weed while they had a hardy laugh at her expense.

We arrived, and my heart sank into a state of despair. I slowly walked into the house, which was filled with thick clouds of cigarette smoke. I could hardly breathe. The music was playing so loud I expected the cops to be called.

I could not stay in that atmosphere. I was about to be sick. I needed fresh air, so I went outside.

Angus followed me outside, and with a frown on his face he said, "You act like you're not enjoying yourself."

"No, I'm not," I answered. "I shouldn't have come here. Angus, I'm just not this kind of person anymore."

He snapped back, "You have only been gone six months, and now you think you're better than we are? Those #$@&%*! Kurtzes have brainwashed you."

"Angus, the Kurtzes are very kind people and take good care of me. For the first time in my life, I know what a real family is like. They love me. They take me to church, and I've been learning about a man called Jesus."

Angus face turned bloodred as his blood pressure began to boil. His blood shot eyes pierced darts of hatred at me. He began screaming so loudly that I thought my eardrums would burst. With bitter words, he began to make a mockery of Jesus, God, and the church. With the sneering look of a mad dog, he got in my face and said, "Well, I can see it didn't take long for them to fill your mind with that religious garbage."

I was so scared I didn't say a word. I knew what Angus was capable of doing. Angus was like Jekyll and Hyde. Most of the time he was kind and to this day my favorite brother, but when his anger got the best of him, he turned into a monster.

I found a shady spot under a tree and sat down on the ground, picking up dirt and letting it flow gently through my fingers. My thoughts were, *Jeanette, you're just a piece of dirt. Good for nothing. You mess up everything. You had a good home and walked away from it.* Minutes seemed like hours as I waited to try to get to a phone. The party was still going on in the house. Alcohol and drugs were flowing freely. Finally, without anyone paying attention to me, I was able to call the Kurtzes, and they came after me. At last I was back in my haven of safety. Home sweet home.

The next morning when I arrived at school. I noticed a group of kids gathered in a circle. They were laughing, whispering, and pointing their fingers at me. I walked into the classroom, but before I could sit down the teacher said to me, "Jeanette, Mrs. Strong wants to see you in her office."

Mrs. Strong was the vice principal of the school, so naturally, I thought I was in trouble for something. I did not know that the school faculty was trying to protect me from the ridicule of the other students.

Unbeknownst to me, my siblings had been on the national news headlines. The County had spread out a wide search net for two suspects in a murder case. The names of the two suspects were Angus and Adelia Jones.

My mind started spinning like a top. I had been with them last night. They were planning and plotting this horrible thing with me in the house. I later learned that they went to a man's house to rob him. Things didn't go as planned, so they killed him in cold blood. Trying to dispose of the evidence, they poured gasoline on the house and the man. They struck a match, and *boom*. Up in flames it went.

I could hardly believe these two people were my brother and sister. How could they commit such an unconscionable act of violence?

After that stressful day, I was so thankful to be home with the Kurtzes. I went to bed early that night from sheer exhaustion. My emotions were all over the place. I felt like my insides were shattered into a million tiny pieces. I lay there in silence, and before I knew it, I had drifted off to sleep, saying, "I'm home. Home sweet home."

CHAPTER 6

THOU SHALL NOT STEAL

The horrifying murder my brother and sister committed just pushed me over the edge. I felt like a pressure cooker about to explode. All the dominos in my game of life were falling one after the other. My nerves felt like electricity was flowing through them at the speed of light. I couldn't handle the stress. I had a nervous breakdown and ended up in the hospital.

During this shocking experience, the Kurtz family came to see me every single day. They went out of their way to show me how much they loved me. They wanted me back in their care as soon as possible. When I was finally released from the hospital, they welcomed me home with open arms.

Terri Kurtz, their daughter, and I began building a tight relationship. She was kind, loving, and accepted me as her new sibling. We were sisters. We began doing things together. We cooked meals, baked cookies, and of course, went shopping. One day Mom Barbara said, "Why don't you two go shopping?" She gave us money, and we headed to the mall.

This was certainly a new experience for me. I had real money to spend on whatever I wanted. We went into a store to look around. I wanted to get something special for Mom Barbara. I searched intently until I discovered an item I thought she would like. I picked the item up and slipped it into my bag. My thoughts were, *Why buy something when you can get it free?* After all, this had been my mentality my entire life.

We left the store. I was smiling like the Cheshire cat in Alice in Wonderland. I was so excited with the gift I had gotten I just had to show it to Terri. I proudly announced that I had stolen it. She got very angry, and in a stern voice she said, "The Kurtz family does not steal! If you want something, you buy it." She continued to speak to me as forcefully as she had done when scolding me for my act of thievery. "Now we're going back into that store, and you are going to put the item back." I reluctantly put my stolen prize back where I had taken it from. We walked out of the store. I just couldn't understand why Terri wouldn't allow me to keep the treasured gift I was so very proud of.

When we got back home Terri told her mom about the episode. My thoughts were, *Well, here comes the screaming and the cursing.*

Instead Mom Barbara asked me in a soft, kind, voice, "Jeanette, why did you steal from the store? You had money."

I stuttered, "Well, I wanted to keep the money, and at the same time I wanted to get something special for you. I wanted to show you how much I love you."

I did not see the wrong in this as my biological mother had trained me to steal from the rich and give to the poor, even though the Kurtzes were not poor by any means. I was still acting out, as if I were Robin Hood and his Merry Men.

To my surprise, there was no screaming, cursing, or black-and-blue beatings. Instead, for the first time in my life, there were only kind words of constructive teaching. Mom Barbara wanted me to understand the difference between right and wrong.

She read to me from the Bible—*the Ten Commandments*, Exodus 20:1–17. When she got to verse 15 she paused, looked me straight in the eyes, and I saw nothing but love and kindness. Mrs. Kurtz patted me on the hand and continued with, "Let's read verse 15 together. It says, *'Thou Shall Not Steal.'* She shared with me that love could be shown in different ways without breaking God's laws or man's laws. We prayed together, and I asked God for forgiveness. From that day forward, I never did steal another thing. My life of crime ended right then and there.

CHAPTER 7

NO MORE SLEEPING UNDER A BRIDGE

I will never forget the day the Kurtz family asked me if I would like for them to adopt me. I was so excited I could hardly breathe. I didn't have to think twice before I enthusiastically answered, "Of course, yes!" The cheerleader in me wanted to jump up and down, do a few cartwheels, wave my arms high in the air, and spell out the words, "Yes, yes, yes!"

At this time, the laws in the state of Texas allowed a child of a certain age to say who they wanted to live with. Without a doubt, I chose the home of the Kurtzes.

The Kurtzes went to an attorney to start the adoption procedures. The attorney's advice was for them *not* to go through with the adoption. He said that statistics showed that a child like me would not respond to living a moral and proper life. He further stated that I would prove to be nothing but trouble and would become a major headache for them.

The Kurtzes were determined to go through with the process. They felt like I had been sent to them by God. Therefore, they disregarded the attorney's advice and started the adoption proceedings.

One of the first things that had to be done was to get my birth certificate. When we got the certificate, I was shocked to see that I was born August 28, 1960. My biological mother told me that I was born October 28, 1960. It was yet another stab at the heart of hurt and disappointment. How could a mother not know the day you were born? The rejection I felt was unsurmountable. It haunted me for years.

However, my nature was to always look for the silver lining in a cloud. It was difficult of course. The clouds in my life, up until this point, had always been dark, gloomy, filled with frightening lightning strikes and tornado-like winds. Now that I had someone to celebrate with me, I decided I would celebrate my birthday on both of the dates my mother had given me, the true and the false. I would be like Alice in Wonderland. I had fallen down a rabbit hole and could celebrate all I wanted. Of course, this was dependent upon the judicial system and the outcome of the adoption proceedings. I prayed feverishly for a positive outcome.

It was as if a snail walking through peanut butter must have been in charge of the US Mail on this particular route. It seemed like a lifetime for all the paperwork and documents to get through the court's red tape.

The day finally came for our court date. When Dad Richard, Mom Barbara, and I entered the courtroom, it was full of people. A dead silence filled the room. It was so silent that if a pen had dropped on the floor, it would have sounded like a grenade had gone off. We sat down quiet as a mouse. I sat with my hands crossed in my lap. I was shaking so hard that I was sure everyone could hear my teeth chattering. The only thing that could stop the adoption would be if my biological mother should show up in court. She had been informed by the judicial system of the potential adoption. My stomach was tied up in knots, and I felt like I was going to throw up at any minute. My heart pounded each time the door opened and someone entered the room. I was so hoping she would not come and contest the new gift of life that was being given me.

Our case number was called. I took a deep breath, and side by side we all went forward to stand before the judge. I trembled as I walked toward the man who had the power to either give or take away from me the new life I so desired. I was short in stature and the desk in front of me seemed as though it was ten feet tall, towering high above me. When I looked up at the judge, it seemed as if he was sitting high upon a throne.

The judge read over the adoption papers and asked questions pertaining to our case. Silence filled the air as he slowly thumbed through the paperwork. I knew this man had the power to say yes or no to our request. It seemed forever before he picked up his mallet and slammed it against his desk. The loud thud would forever echo in my ears as the judge finally said, "This court awards this child, Jeanette Jones, to the custody of Mr. and Mrs. Richard Kurtz." The legal documents were signed, and my adoption papers were finalized.

I was so excited it seemed as if I just floated out of the courtroom. We left the courthouse, walked outside and down the long line of steps. The air seemed so fresh and clean, and the sun shone brighter than ever before. My newly adoptive parents held my hands. Mom Barbara was on one side, and Dad Richard on the other. I cannot describe the feeling of overwhelming joy I felt as we walked side by side. To paraphrase a quote given in a speech by the great Martin Luther King Jr., "Free at last! Free at last! Thank God Almighty, [I] was free at last!"

We climbed into the car and with a sigh of relief, an indescribable peace filled my soul. I would be going "home" with my new family. I would have my own room, a place to hang my clothes, take a bath, brush my teeth, sit down, and eat a meal, and all the wonderful and beautiful things a "normal" family experienced every day. My holocaust had ended, and heaven lay before me. As I took in all the thoughts of my newfound future, I knew at that moment that there would be no more sleeping under a bridge.

CHAPTER 8

DEFENSELESS

Early that morning, I struggled to get out of bed. It had been one of those sleepless nights fighting off horrid nightmares. I stumbled to the kitchen and was greeted by the smell of strong coffee. Thankfully, my sweet mom had made a pot of coffee before leaving for the office. I sat down at the table with coffee cup in hand. The aroma floated up to my nostrils as I took my first sip. I couldn't resist the chocolate doughnuts sitting on the table, so I allowed myself just one.

I picked up the morning paper and began to read. My eyes fell upon an article that stood out in big, bold, black letters:

WOMAN'S BODY FOUND BEHIND
JACKSON'S CAR WASH

Homicide detectives are trying to identify a woman's body found near a trash bin

> in the rear of a self-service carwash near Macon and Jackson. The victim was found just before noon by a passer-by who called the police. The victim was a Caucasian woman who assumed to be in her twenties. The deceased woman's hands were bound behind her back. She was naked and wrapped in a blanket according to LT David Martello from the homicide unit. Homicide detectives are awaiting a report from the Shelby County Medical Examiner's office on the cause of her death.

After reading the article, I was overwhelmed with a tremendous sadness as I thought about the family who would be faced with this horrible tragedy. It left me with a sinking feeling in the pit of my stomach.

I finished my coffee and started to make my plans for the day that lay ahead. I walked out of the kitchen, never dreaming that the newspaper article and this terrible event would actually affect me. I didn't know at the time a knock would come to our door with horrifying news. Yet it did arrive, and I learned the woman I was reading about was my sister Abbigail. I was in shock. I don't remember much more about that day except I felt I was stumbling through a horrible storm.

An investigation of the crime ensued, and being next of kin I was, of course, privy to the gruesome facts surrounding my sister's death. I remember sitting in the kitchen and reading the detailed report given to me by the police. It was so horrible I could hardly believe it. Abbigail had been brutally murdered. Her hands were tied behind her back. She was left naked and wrapped in a blanket. She had been tortured unmercifully, beaten to a pulp, and was virtually unrecognizable. Objects had been forced up into her vagina and rectum. I felt weak and sick as I forced myself to read about the hideous nightmare my beloved sister had suffered at the hands of her assailant.

After reading the report, my hands started shaking uncontrollably. I dropped the paper and watched as it floated in slow motion to the floor. I became disoriented and had a sense of being out of control.

Everything around me suddenly began to fade away, as if awaking from a dream, or in this case, a terrible nightmare. A wave of nausea swept through me, and cold chills ran down my spine, leaving me with a shiver that I can only describe as the chill of death.

I ran to the bathroom and fought with the nausea, yet I ended up vomiting all that I had just eaten. I can recall the cold floor beneath me as I began to shake my head in disbelief. The only word coming to mind was, *No! This could not be. No, no, no, not Abbigail.*

My head was spinning. I felt as if I were in a rudderless boat thrashing downstream in white water rapids. I seemed to be hitting every jagged rock and boulder along the way. As I was being carried downstream, I knew the doomed boat was being ripped apart. I became fully aware that I was taking on water and I was in imminent danger. Without help, I knew I would be consumed by the turbulent waters.

I was desperate. I needed someone to toss me an oar so I could navigate the boat into calmer waters. I knew I must take charge of my life, take the oar in my hands, and steer my vessel to safety. I could not allow my boat to go over the waterfalls that surely lay ahead. I sat on the floor and cried out hysterically in deep wailing sobs.

To the average person, this may seem a normal response to deep duress, but this in fact came as a shock to me. I had not shed a tear in a long time, except for the day I received my salvation when I was born again. My stepfather always tormented me, "Big girls don't cry." I suppose I developed somewhat of a hard heart for the sake of survival.

It took a tragic event such as this to finally bring a torrent of my tears to the surface. Tears escaped from the prison they had been held in for many years.

I had learned from a scientific study that the normal response to high emotion is crying. The emotion of crying looks very simple on paper. However, it is one of the most complicated responses that are a vital part of human existence. Emotions are very complex, and every individual has their own emotional fingerprint.

It is said that humans are the only living things on earth that shed tears when they are overcome with emotion. It is a natural response to things we are faced with in life. Not only is it normal to cry, but it is also healthy. Studies have shown that tears, resulting from emotion, have a different chemistry than tears obtained by simply irritants in the air.

In this scientific study, I learned that emotional tears were found to have high levels of toxins, which the body rids itself of after a good cry. Our bodies build up these toxins while preparing for the crying episode. The body then releases these toxins by way of our tear ducts. It is no wonder that I threw up. My body must have been filled with nothing but toxins.

After much investigation, the facts vital to the case came to surface. Abbigail had chosen to fall prey to her addictions and live within a darkness that swallows you but seldom spits you out. All the choices she had made brought her to the end of her life, by being brutally tortured and murdered. Yet no matter the life we live, no matter the mistakes we make, no one deserves to die the way my beloved sister did. At this time, I felt like the police department did not make Abbigail a priority as they had seen this all too many times. They were of no help to our family in our pursuit to find her murderer. They looked at this murder as just one less junky and one less prostitute off the streets. They were very familiar with Abbigail as she was arrested on a regular basis. She had drug possession charges against her, also theft, and the list goes on and on, longer than Santa's Christmas list.

At that time, I felt the police had bigger and better fish to fry. She, to the police, was no more than trash thrown out with the rest of the garbage. She was one less person to deal with, dragging in and out of their cells. Today, I know that this is not the case, and I am certain they did the best they could to solve this murder. Rather than spend the time and money it would take to follow through with most likely a lengthy investigation, her murder was marked, "Case Closed."

After Abbigail's death, the horrifying images, the gruesome details, and the helpless feelings of not resolving her murder continued to force its way into my thoughts day in and day out. I kept having flashbacks of her being wrapped in a dirty blanket all alone, with no one to comfort or hold her.

I had to force my mind to go elsewhere. I would close my eyes and allow myself to drift back into the memories of the times when I sat on Abbigail's lap. She would tell me of how she sheltered and protected me when I was a baby and young child.

She told me she would wrap me in a blanket and embrace me in her loving arms; otherwise, I was completely neglected. She wanted to protect me from all the dangers she knew I would face in the no-too-distant future. She and my sister Adelia were being molested by our stepfather, and soon I would be exposed to the same tragic events.

Thinking back, I recall on many occasions, Abbigail would take her bath, go to her room, only to find our stepfather lying at the foot of her bed. The door to her room would then close. Abbigail was a fighter and would do everything in her power to overcome her attacker, yet her molester was just too strong. She learned early in life that sick people will take advantage of you, abuse you, and there would be nothing you could do to stop it. Sadly, in the end, she lost her fight.

Abbigail knew this was happening also to my middle sister Adelia and so would surely befall me. In our attempts to tell our mother what was happening, we would get punished for making up stories. She did not believe us. Perhaps she did believe, yet she was too afraid of our stepfather to confront him.

The bottom line, I made every effort to avoid my stepfather when he was assaulting my sisters. He was sure to remind us that any further attempts to tell our mother would end her life. His threats were real, and we knew the heartless animal we lived with would, with no remorse, kill our precious mother.

Abbigail left home at an early age to escape this hell. Abbigail loved me and wanted to warn me about my daunting future. She gave me a safety pin and told me to keep it, and if he came after me in the night, to stick him as hard as I could where the sun don't shine. This unfortunately proved ineffective when he began his assaults on me.

It was not difficult to understand how Abbigail's life had ended up so tragically. I could not blame her. After all, we were born and raised in the whirlwind of a distorted and twisted reality. We were left in the devastation of the debris that came from the daily storms in our lives.

We never knew which way the winds of disaster would take us. Life's winds were as strong as pounding raindrops and deadly hailstones. The only solitude I could find in this tragedy was that Abbigail no longer had to bear the pain of physical and mental hurt, shame, disgust, and abuse that had pierced her mind and body for so many years.

Sometime later, we learned her murder was because she had witnessed the murder of another person. Tragically the victim of that murder found they were defenseless and paid the price.

I am often reminded that Abbigail was no more than a victim of circumstance. She was just simply a small child who was forced into acts to which she was totally defenseless. She had lived her life unable to defend herself and sadly she lost her life *defenseless*.

CHAPTER 9

My Knight in Shining Armor

I graduated in 1979 from Richland High School, Birdville ISD. I will never forget that day standing in line waiting for them to call my name. I was so excited to walk across that stage to receive my diploma. Finally, I heard them call "Jeanette Jones." I didn't walk slowly! I practically flew across that stage and was so thankful that my cap didn't fall off.

After graduation, the school district encouraged me to go to college to become a physical education teacher, which by the way, was my dream. I didn't have the confidence academically that I needed. I had lost so much of the basics because of my dysfunctional childhood. Nevertheless, I decided to take their advice and go.

Some of my friends from the high school basketball team were going also. My mom, Barbara, along with some of the other mothers, made arrangements to take us to Stephen F. Austin University in Nacogdoches, Texas.

Dayna Farmer, Karen Pitchford, and I loved the university, and all agreed this would be the place for us. All three of us were accepted, so off to college we went.

College was a completely different world. The campus was large and jam-packed with students, teachers, and support staff. The list of college courses to choose from was so lengthy, it made my head swim. My first few days on campus included school orientations, dormitory rules and regulations, and of course becoming acquainted with my roommate and fellow classmates. I was on the run every day; go here, be there. All freshmen were housed in separate residence halls from their upper classmen. Every freshman classmate I ran into was just as disoriented as I was. We were like mice running through a maze, trying to find our way around and become familiar with our new surroundings. Naturally, we all missed home at first and were a bit frightened. There were, however, senior counselors in the dorms to give us the assurance we needed that all would be well. As we settled into our new life of home away from home, we calmed down and recognized what a wonderful experience and adventure lay before. After all was said and done, I must admit it was such great fun.

I struggled with my classes the first semester. Even though I wasn't the sharpest pencil in the box, I was the most determined. I was placed on academic probation because my grades fell short of passing. It made me feel really bad, yet I was doing everything in my power to be successful. I did not want to fail my classes, so I decided to talk with my professors. Graciously, they taught me how to study for tests. My mom, Barbara, also extended some help. She showed me how to write papers. She also helped me to improve on my academic skills in areas where I needed help. Finally, things began to look up for me.

The Birdville School District said they would hire me to coach basketball when I finished my education. I got my basics at Tarrant County Junior College during the summer and completed my education in three years. I majored in generic special education and became a physical education teacher. I began coaching basketball, which was my true love.

During my college years I was also involved in the Baptist Student Union on campus. We went on a few mission trips, including local events, which were very exciting. My life was filled with school and BSU meetings.

As far as dating, it wasn't a priority for me. College, BSU, and basketball were my loves. My family teased me about marriage and said if I ever married, it would be to a basketball. I dated some guys in college, but there was always something about them I didn't like. Therefore, I wouldn't go out with them again. I'm sure it wasn't the young men's fault. I think deep down I was afraid of them because of what I had gone through growing up. My childhood left me with low self-esteem and fear of rejection.

Each day I looked forward to school and going to the Baptist Student Union on campus. I was on a committee for Senior Citizen's Outreach Ministries. We went to nursing homes to visit and sing to the residents.

One day I was at the Baptist Student Union on campus, and in walked this young, breathtakingly good-looking, handsome guy. He was a tall drink of water. You get my drift? His name was Gary Golden, and hanging on to his arm like superglue was one of my friends, Lisa. Lisa looked up at him with goo-goo eyes. I could not help but stare at this handsome creature because I had the strangest feeling come over me. It was something I had never experienced before. It actually scared me. I said to myself, "I'm going to marry that guy."

Suddenly I started wearing makeup, fixing my hair, and became very particular in what I wore. I knew I was dressing up for Gary, but I didn't know why. We had not dated, and he was always with Lisa, so it was an unexpected surprise when one day he asked Lisa and me to go to Wendy's for a Frosty. This really confused me. Why would he invite both of us? Maybe he was trying to make up his mind which one of us he liked best. My mind and my emotions were muddled. I thought, *Oh well. I will be just like Scarlett O'Hara in* Gone with the Wind *when she became confused or overwhelmed.* I repeated what she would say, "I'll think about that tomorrow."

Sitting at Wendy's, Gary and I hit it off and talked as if we had known each other forever. I am sure Lisa felt like a third wheel because she couldn't get a word in edgewise. She sighed every once in a while and looked very bored. She sat quietly and sipped on her Frosty. From that day forward, Gary and I were together day and night for three weeks.

On Valentine weekend, our Baptist Student Union was going to Lubbock, Texas, on a mission trip. I was very excited about this trip and was looking forward to spending every moment with Gary. I could picture myself on the bus sitting close to Gary and laying my head on his shoulder. To my bitter disappointment, I was put on one bus and Gary and Lisa were on another bus. I had to fight back the tears as I had done many time before. Tears still did not come easy for me. I bought Gary a teddy bear for Valentine. I wrote a note that said "I love you" and pinned it to the bear. I rushed over to his bus before he got on and handed him the bear. Lisa saw me do this, but I really didn't care.

All the way to Lubbock, my mind played ping-pong, the ball bouncing back and forth, chanting, *He loves me— no, he loves Lisa. What is he thinking about the teddy bear? Was I foolish to have given him the bear? What must he be thinking?*

It seemed like it took the bus forever to get to Lubbock, but we finally did arrive. I maneuvered my way down the aisle of the bus as quickly as I could. I wanted to see Gary and his smiling face. I retrieved my belongings and made my way through the crowds. My mind was being bombarded by thoughts, *Gary, Gary, Gary*. Then his name would be cancelled out as I heard the words, *Lisa, Lisa, Lisa*. The aggravating thoughts continued, *He does not belong to you, he loves her.*

Then I saw him in the distance. He was headed straight toward me. I stopped dead in my tracks, making sure my eyes weren't deceiving me. I blinked and blinked again. I was not hallucinating. Before I really realized what was happening, Gary grabbed me up in his arms, pulled me very close, and held me tightly. I couldn't breathe. I was in ecstasy.

Other than my adoptive dad, Richard, for the first time in my life I was in the arms of a man and felt love, comfort, and safety. In Gary's arms, I felt like I was being bathed in an ocean of liquid love, sweeping away all the horrible things I had endured in my young life. Thoughts were rushing through my head like the Colorado River, fast and furious.

The days and nights in Lubbock were fantastic. Gary and I were like two peas in a pod. The week flew by, and we were going home the next day. On our last night there, we walked hand in hand and found a cozy private place to sit and talk. It was a warm night, although a gentle breeze was blowing. The sky looked as if a giant hand had flung millions of bright stars across the heavens.

I lay my head on Gary's shoulder. I was in perfect peace, knowing in my heart this was where I belonged. Then Gary handed me a small box. I opened it, and there was a sparkling diamond necklace. I was in total shock as Gary said, "Let me put this on you."

After fastening the clasp on my necklace, he turned me around and looked straight into my eyes. His eyes were gleaming as he told me how much he loved me, and asked me to marry him. My head was full of fireworks bursting forth like the Fourth of July. I could not believe the words I had just heard. *He loves me. He really loves me*. I could feel it in his touch, see it in his eyes, and hear it in his soft voice. I was like a giant iceberg, melting away with every beat of my heart. Soon there would be nothing but a puddle of water.

At last my knight in shining armor had ridden up on his white horse, swept me up into his arms, and was going to carry me off to his castle in the sky to live happily ever after. Of course, I said, "Yes!"

I could hardly wait to get home to tell my parents that Gary had asked me to marry him. I was disappointed as the news of our engagement went over like a lead balloon. My parents did not share our enthusiasm. After all, we had only known each other for three weeks. Surely, I was just infatuated with this handsome young man, and it would be a short-lived admiration. Last, but not least, they were greatly concerned about my academic future. They insisted I must finish my college education before they would give us their blessing.

We were so much in love and so secure in our decision to marry, we happily agreed to work hard, finish our educations, and get our degrees. We counted the days.

Finally, the big day arrived, our wedding day! I felt like Cinderella going to the ball as I put on my wedding dress and stood before the minister. Gary seemed more handsome than usual. It truly was a day to celebrate and bask in the beauty of it all. We exchanged vows and placed our wedding rings on each other's fingers. At last, the minister made the announcement, "I present to you Mr. and Mrs. Gary Golden. You may kiss the bride."

Gary gently pulled me to himself and gave me a kiss that I will cherish all the rest of my life. I had met and married my knight in shining armor. We are still happily married and celebrated our thirty-sixth anniversary in 2018. Every day has been one long honeymoon.

Oh Happy Days I Captured My Knight in Shining Armor

Gary and I on Our Wedding Day

CHAPTER 10

God Is My Anchor

After Gary and I got married, we moved to Houston, Texas. Gary continued his education by attending the University of Houston, College of Optometry, in pursuit of his degree in eye care. During this time, I taught special education at Clover Leaf Elementary School. I also taught special education at North Shore Elementary School.

Gary and I were happily married and enjoying our life in Houston. It seemed like the first two years of marriage simply flew by. My sister, Terri, had married. My brother, Kevin, was a senior in high school and would soon be graduating. My parents were getting ready to sell their floral business and retire. They were moving to Camden, Arkansas, to care for their aging parents.

Summer turned into fall, and fall turned into winter. Christmas was just around the corner and we were looking forward to going home for the holidays. It was December

16, 1984, a very cold day. Gary was putting together the exercise equipment he had given me for Christmas.

The telephone rang, and it was my adoptive dad, Richard. He was calling to see how we were doing and was looking forward to our visit over the Christmas holidays.

My parents were very involved in their church and loved to host parties and entertain. Dad told me they were having a Sunday School Christmas party the next day. Mom was decorating the Christmas tree with multicolored lights, tree trimmings, and our favorite ornaments. Dad said Mom had baked for days, getting ready for this special occasion. We had a wonderful conversation, said our "I love yous" and then our "goodbyes."

The next morning, Gary left for the clinic, and I left for work at the school. I entered my classroom with the sounds of boisterous, laughing, giggling children. Excitement filled the air, the children knowing they would soon be released for the Christmas holidays.

I was wrapping Christmas presents for my students when my name was called on the school intercom, asking me to come to the office. It was not unusual for a teacher to be summoned to the office for one reason or another, so I thought very little of it. I was wondering what parent or child I had offended or angered. These were natural thoughts for a teacher.

I walked in the office and saw Gary standing there. He had a horrible look on his face. I knew immediately something terrible had happened. My mind raced. I could hardly breathe. "Gary, what is it? What has happened?"

Gary was almost pale knowing he would be the one to deliver yet another hard blow. He gently pulled me to himself and whispered in my ear, "I have bad news, my love."

My dad, Richard, had been killed.

My mind went into a tailspin. I was filled with strong emotions of shock and disbelief. I felt hysteria would consume me. I wanted to run, to hide, and to do anything to keep from facing the horrible truth of my dad's death. I went through the motions of packing and loading the car as if in a haze.

We left Houston for our drive to my parents' house in Fort Worth, Texas. I cried all the way. My thoughts drifted back to the conversation with Dad over the phone just the day before. I never dreamed that this would be the last time I would talk to him. I was devastated.

When we arrived home, Gary and I made our way through the Sunday school Christmas party crowd. They had come for a celebration, but upon hearing the news, stayed to support Mom. Mom and I met somewhere in the haze of horror that clouded the rooms so familiar to us. Mom's eyes were filled with tears. She stretched out her loving arms, and we fell into each other's embrace. My mom was in a state of shock and was consumed with overwhelming grief.

Somehow I began to compose myself and found out from my mom that Dad had gone out into the garage to work on his van. He jacked up the vehicle and got under it to do some maintenance. The jack broke, fell on top of him and crushed him to death. To her misfortune, my sister Terri was the person who found Dad. She immediately called 911. The EMTs were not able to revive him.

During Christmas there was always a high rate of suicides and murders. In order to rule out any sort of foul play or unlikely suicide attempt, we had to wait for the officials to finish their investigation before we could have a funeral for Dad.

After Dad's funeral, reality began to sink in. I simply could not wrap my mind around his death. He was the gentlest man I had ever known. He never raised his voice and always told us how much he loved us.

The dark hours and days that followed seemed like a blur. I was like a fish out of water, flipping around on dry ground. I was just trying to breathe, trying to survive. I tried desperately to fight off the dreary cloud of sorrow, sadness, and depression. Completely grief-stricken, I fell into a state of hopelessness.

The human brain is programmed to adjust itself to life changes and situations. My mind was not adjusting at all. I felt like I was on the sinking ship *Titanic*, with no hope of rescue in sight. I was trying to avoid the huge chunks of icebergs bobbing up and down all around me in the freezing waters. Like the *Titanic*, physically and emotionally I was being ripped apart. I was sinking like lead, fast and furiously.

Out of my desperation, I cried out to God to save me from the cold waters of death. I had already had a nervous breakdown in earlier years. I did not want to go down that road again. Gary and I prayed. Our friends and church family reached out to as well, throwing us life preservers of God's amazing grace. The waters did not calm all at once, and though our ship seemed to be sinking we found God to be our anchor in the storm.

Hebrews 6:18–19 (Amplified Bible) reads,

> So that by two unchangeable things [His promise and His oath] in which it is impossible for God to lie, we who have fled [to Him] for refuge would have strong encouragement and indwelling strength to hold tightly to the hope set before us. This hope [this confident assurance] we have as an anchor of the soul [it cannot slip and it cannot break down under whatever pressure bears upon it]—a safe and steadfast hope that enters within the veil [of the heavenly temple, that most Holy Place in which the very presence of God dwells].

CHAPTER 11

FOOTPRINTS IN THE SAND

In 1986, Gary graduated from Optometry School. We moved to Center, Texas, where Gary worked alongside his brother, Dr. Dixon Golden, at the Golden Eye Center. These names reminded me of a James Bond movie. I think I called their practice "The Golden Eye." Ha-ha!

After getting settled in our new community, Gary and I decided to start our family. I will never forget the day it was confirmed that I was expecting our first baby. I was overjoyed with the thrill and excitement of becoming a mother. Like any new expectant mother, I immediately became attached to this tiny person that I would soon bring into this great big world of ours.

Gary and I could not have been happier. Those nine months of my life were fabulous. Then the day of my delivery came, and my world came crashing down. I hit rock bottom. The birthing pains began, and what a startling awakening that was. Gary rushed me to the Nacogdoches Medical Center. The day was October 8, 1987, when Robert Golden, Jr. arrived.

However, labor and delivery did not happen without complications. Rob weighed eight pounds and six ounces. His sheer size demanded an intense and grueling physical pushing on my part to bring Rob into the world.

We had been cautioned in birthing class of the dangers of using forceps in delivery due to the chances of causing brain damage. Therefore, we opted out, and I chose to endure to the bitter end!

Once the baby's head cleared the birth canal, I thought the worst was over, but not so. I was told that his shoulder was the same diameter as his head. The baby was, in a sense, stuck, and so was I. I listened to the doctor, attempting to come up with a solution to the dilemma. He stated that a C-section was not an option because things had gone too far to attempt any surgical procedure.

The decision was made. They would have to break his shoulder. By the time the ordeal was over, I looked like I had been run over by a Mack truck, and I felt like it too. I can only imagine how my precious baby must have suffered.

Not only did Rob suffer an injury during delivery, I also broke my sternum. As a result, I was not able to breastfeed my baby. It took several weeks for both of us to heal.

Soon after delivery, I began to have a number of medical issues. I was in a lot of pain in my back and female organs. My lower abdomen was so tender to the touch that the slightest movement would bring me to tears. I went to several doctors, and there seemed to be no answers as to why I was having so much pain.

Most people did not know, including some of my doctors, that I was sexually abused at a very early age. The initial diagnosis was that I had contracted some type of syphilis. The reaction of the medical professionals was disappointing. I felt men and women in this field would not be so quick to judge. Seeing their facial expressions and demeanor, I was most obviously labeled a whore in their eyes. I was too ashamed to tell them what had happened to me. I am sure they were shocked because all tests came back negative on syphilis or any other sexually transmitted disease.

I went to several doctors and still did not have an answer as to why I was having abdominal pain. I chose to deal with the pain. Gary and I prayed about it and decided we should have another baby. After all, I felt great while I was expecting. I quit going to doctors concerning the pain. Instead, I went to my ob-gyn and was told that everything was normal physically and I could go forward with my happy plan.

However, before I could get home from the doctor's office, the lab called. I was stunned as I heard the voice on the other end of the phone tell me that I had Stage 4 Cancer of the cervix. The highest stage would be 5, so stage 4 was obviously not a good report.

You can imagine the shockwave that ran through my veins. I had just been told by my ob-gyn that everything looked great. The good news had been, "Go home and make babies!"

I sat starring into space as the nurse on the phone told me that I needed to return to the office because my life was in grave danger. I had just been told everything was wonderful in one breath, and with the very next breath, I was told I was in grave danger. You can just imagine my state of confusion.

My next step was to make an appointment with an oncologist to understand more clearly what I was facing. Unfortunately, this doctor also confirmed my initial diagnosis, and I was scheduled for surgery.

My grandmother and my husband were my only support at this time. My grandmother had just lost her daughter at a very early age to Hodgkin's disease. The daughter left behind two sons, which my grandmother would now raise. Not many people knew the battle I was facing, but my faithful grandmother was there to pray for me. She offered a great deal of support in many other ways as well.

It had been an arduous undertaking in survival to get to the place where I was at this point. I had just begun a new chapter in my life. Now I was asking myself, "Is this the ending of the book?"

I remember the time when our family was at the beach and the feel of the sand squishing between my toes. Perhaps you have built a sand castle on the beach. You spent hours and hours creating a unique sculpture of which you were very proud, yet when the tide rolled in, you could only stand by helplessly and watch as the prize castle was swept out to sea.

As I dealt with the incoming tidal waves of gloom and despair spoken over me, it seemed that my sand castle was about to be swept into the depths of the ocean. Slowly the grains of sand would sink, down, down, down into the bottomless abyss.

At this point, I felt confused, uncertain, and alone in my search for answers. I came upon a story about God's presence, and I have frequently turned to it for strength over the years.

The story is about a man walking along a beach with the Lord when suddenly many scenes from his life begin to flash across the sky. In each scene, he notices footprints in the sand, one belonging to him and one belonging to the Lord. Sometimes the man sees only one set of footprints, which were present during the lowest periods of his life. He is distraught to see only one when in anguish, sorrow, or defeat. When his life was on a normal keel, he saw the two set of footprints.

The man cries out to the Lord, "You promised, Lord, that if I followed You, You would walk with me always. But I notice that there are only one set of footprints in the sand during the most traumatic periods of my life. Why, when I needed You the most, were You not there for me?"

> The Lord replied, "My precious, precious child. I love you and I would never, never leave you during your times of trials and suffering. Where you see only one set of footprints, it was then that I carried you."

When I think of this story, I hear God saying, "Jeanette, I have not left you. When there is just one set of footprints, know that I am carrying you."

My next step in dealing with the news of stage 4 cancer was to seek help at MD Anderson Hospital in Houston, Texas. After many tests, I was told that my issues were caused by the early childhood sexual activity. Again, I felt shame, even though I had no control over the unsolicited, undesirable acts of aggression forced upon me.

The only good thing about this condition was that it was found in one central location. I was told that I could undergo a procedure called conization of the cervix, which meant they would remove a cone-shaped section of the uterus. This would require a visit to the clinic every three weeks for one year and then once a year for ten years.

I was also told that if I would do exactly as I was instructed, I might be able to have another child. The catch was that I would be unable to carry full term. The physicians would have to surgically suture me together on the inside in order to hold the baby at all. Also, total bed rest would be required.

My greatest testimony is that God intervened, and none of the above happened. The Great Physician had not only carried me through the sandy shores of impending doom, but as He carried me, He touched me and made me whole. There were no more depressing diagnostic procedures to adhere to.

I had two more boys, one right after the other. I call them my miracle babies. Kurtis Golden was born in 1991 and Andrew Golden in 1992. Once the boys were born, the doctors recommended that I have a complete hysterectomy because they expected the cancer would come back and affect my ovaries. It was all right with me because God and I had proven the medical profession wrong. I had two wonderful babies that no one ever expected I would be able to bring into this world.

I had one sister who developed ovarian cancer and one sister developed colon cancer due to the years of sexual abuse. God graciously spared me. I am a survivor. I am cancer free. And God is faithful!

When I think back upon these events, I hear God say, "Jeanette, I have not left you. When there is just one set of footprints, know that I am carrying you."

My Miracle Babies Pictured (left to right)
Rob, Kurtis and Andrew Golden

CHAPTER 12

THE TAPESTRY

Gary bought his brother's clinic in Hemphill, Texas, in 1989. The name of the clinic is Hemphill Eye Clinic. We moved from Center, Texas, to Hemphill, Texas. We settled into our new home and new lifestyle. Hemphill is where we still reside today.

In 1995, I was saddened to be facing some very serious medical conditions once again. I was struggling with multiple illnesses. I had gone to several doctors, trying to find reasons why I had severe weakness in my hands and arms. I was dropping everything I tried to pick up or hold on to. I was suffering with excruciating pain in my back and legs. The chronic pain was affecting me mentally. I was tormented and bombarded with the thought, *Your cancer has come back.* The battle was raging in my mind day and night.

Until I met the Kurtzes, became a born-again Christian, and met and married my sweet husband Gary, I felt as if my life's story had been painted on a dirty canvas and smeared with dirt and grime. Those days were behind, and I had begun anew. Now I faced a new challenge.

In the midst of mental conflict, I began to meditate on the good things in my life. I thought, *My life is like a complex yet beautiful tapestry*. I began to visualize the different colored threads running through the elegant tapestry God had been fabricating.

There were thoughts of my adoptive parents, adoptive siblings, and the lovely colors each of them had woven into my life. Gary certainly had woven stunning threads into the tapestry as well. The threads that each of my sons had woven into my tapestry was indescribable. I thought of the many miracles God had graced me with.

I realized, however, one thread in the fabric was loose, making the entire piece fragile and delicate. I also realized the pulling of this one thread could unravel the whole beautiful tapestry. The thread was being pulled and tugged upon, and the tapestry was coming apart quickly.

Oh, how I wished that somehow the threads would hold together. Yet it was happening, and now I found myself in a hopeless situation. Again, I was wondering what I could do to stop the unraveling and the loss of this magnificent masterpiece. I was attending First Baptist Church and was a devout church goer and a Christian. I never stopped praying, asking God to help me.

I had three small boys. I loved them unselfishly and unconditionally. I would give my whole life up for them. Yet I found myself losing my patience and not always being the loving mother I should have been. The pain was taking me to a place I did not like. I needed help desperately.

There was a lady in my neighborhood named Pat Speights. She loved to see me coming with my three little boys on our daily walks. One day a friend of Pat's named Betsy Hutcheson joined us. Betsy was a member at Bethany Baptist Church. Betsy was old enough to be my mom and the boy's grandmother. Her heart of compassion saw right through the hurting woman that I was. I was hurting in every way, whether I recognized it or not. Betsy was a quiet, gentle woman of few words. I had only seen Betsy around town but was not at all acquainted with her. This was the first time our paths had crossed and then only briefly.

One day while I was home with the boys, I heard a knock at the door. I opened the door, and there stood a meek little lady. It was Betsy. As we exchanged pleasantries, I sensed an enormous amount of compassion flowing from her heart. She told me that the Lord told her to come by and invite me to the Aglow International Conference in California.

I did not know what to think. She seemed so genuine. She had Aglow pamphlets. She asked me if I would look them over and pray to see if the Lord would have me attend. I thanked her and took the pamphlets and laid them on my countertop.

That same afternoon, a friend and his wife came to our house to eat supper. As they were getting ready to leave, I picked up the pamphlet and asked the couple their thoughts on the Aglow. Their immediate response was, "It is a cult, do not go." In no uncertain terms, they let me know they did not approve of me attending the meeting.

In the meantime, the doctors had finally diagnosed me with fibromyalgia, a sister to lupus. My cancer had not come back. I was not a hypochondriac. I grew up tough and had become a woman of purpose. However, I just couldn't find my way through the maze of all the physical pain.

So I prayed about the Aglow Meeting. I pondered over it for a while and felt God said I should go. What did I have to lose, even if it was a cult? Maybe I could get some help.

I told Gary if it was all right with him, I was going to go. I knew my mother-in-law, Me-Maw, would come and take care of the boys. I also told him that our Baptist church seemed unable to help me, so I might as well attend the Aglow meeting in hopes of finding answers.

I went to California with Betsy Hutcheson, Ginger Giessow, and Ann Smith. I really didn't know any of these women but stayed close to Betsy. We stayed a whole week. This conference changed my life forever. I learned just how much God loved me to send Ms. Betsy to help me.

The first meeting I attended, to say the least, I was shocked when I walked into the auditorium where ten thousand women were praising God. The women were worshipping with their hands raised in the air. Some were dancing, some jumping, clapping their hands, singing in tongues, crying, laughing, and prophesies—"Thus, saith the Lord"—were being spoken.

Well, I knew right then and there I was in the wrong place at the wrong time. After all, I had been taught the things I was seeing did not come from God. I was told that tongues and prophecies died with the New Testament Apostles: Peter, James, John, etc.

On the third day of the conference I became serious with God. The speaker was speaking, and I was talking to God.

"God, is this a cult?"

"God, are all these ten thousand women wrong?"

"God, am I the only person in the room that is right?"

"God, You know my heart, and if this is real, I want it!"

Suddenly, the power of God hit me, and I was immersed into the baptism of the Holy Spirit. I began sliding down out of my seat and was laughing like a drunkard. Believe me I would never have done such a thing as that on my own. After all, I was a doctor's wife and much too sophisticated to make a fool of myself. Yet I did, and at the time I didn't care what anyone thought about me.

I was having a supernatural experience with God. With me on the floor, the minister on the platform began to prophecy. "There is a lady out in the audience who has just had a private conversation with God. Ma'am, you just asked God, 'Is this a cult?' You asked Him for the truth, and He proved it to you by baptizing you in the Holy Ghost. He has also baptized your husband with the Holy Ghost, and when you get home, you will have a new husband."

I knew without a doubt, that prophecy was precisely for me.

Everyone began singing in the Spirit, and I joined in. Out of my mouth began flowing rivers of living water. I was speaking a language I did not know and had not learned. I was speaking in tongues and proud of it. God made a tongue-talking believer of me that night. No one was going to steal this God-breathed gift from me.

Acts 2:4 (King James Version) reads,

> And they were all filled with the Holy Ghost, and began to speak with other tongues, as the Spirit gave them utterance.

I felt like I was wrapped in a heavenly cloud of God's glory, when all of a sudden, I realized all the pain had left my body. I knew at that moment I was miraculously healed! Jesus had touched me!

Psalm 107:20 (King James Version) reads,

> He sent his word, and healed them, and delivered them from their destructions.

Isaiah 53:5 (King James Version) reads,

> But he was wounded for our transgressions, he was bruised for our iniquities: the chastisement of our peace was upon him; and with his stripes we are healed.

I could not wait to get home to see what had happened to Gary. After returning home from California, I told Gary all about the wonderful things that had happened to me. I shared with him that I was filled with the Holy Spirit with the evidence of speaking in tongues.

Then Gary began to tell me that while I was in California, he had gone to a Promise Keeper's Meeting. He told me how God had really ministered to him in a wonderful way at the meeting. He had a fresh, new experience with God but had not received his prayer language. I told Gary to go to his office and begin to praise and worship God, and he would receive. Gary did just as I asked. As he was worshipping God, an overwhelming feeling of great happiness and excitement manifested in his innermost being. As he was basking in the presence of the Lord, a beautiful new language flowed from his mouth. My husband has never been the same.

God filled both of us with His power as the minister had prophesied to me in California. After this unexpected and unimaginable experience with God, the loose threads of my life's tapestry began to weave themselves back together. It became stronger as new colorful threads began to intertwine, knit, and braid themselves together.

My tapestry of life has now been crisscrossed and blended together. I now have a heavenly fashioned, exquisite tapestry to hang on the wall of my life.

Psalm 139:15 (Amplified Bible) reads,

> My frame was not hidden from You, when I was being formed in secret, and intricately and skillfully formed, [as if embroidered with many colors] in the depths of the earth.

CHAPTER 13

MY JOURNEY WITH AGLOW INTERNATIONAL

After the California trip I became a very active member of the Aglow. Someone received the vision, possibly Ms. Betsy and the East Texas Area Board, that Hemphill, Texas, needed an Aglow chapter.

Little did I know God was setting me up for leadership over the Hemphill Aglow. I became president. I was president of the Hemphill Aglow Chapter from 1996 through 2000.

In this new venture, I had to totally follow God. I knew nothing about leading women to a deeper walk with the Lord or having compassion for hurting women.

Aglow was the vehicle God used to bring me to a place of maturity in Him. I was taught to "Be Aglow in the Spirit." I was taught how to pray and how to have faith in God for my health, my community, and whatever else God placed on my heart.

I learned how to be led by the Spirit, how to submit to authority, and how to be humble and not prideful. I learned how to show the love of Jesus to hurting women.

The women of Aglow just simply taught me how to fall in love with Jesus. They caused me to hunger and thirst for His righteousness. They gave me hope, a vision, and a purpose for my life.

Betsy Hutcheson was the woman who affected me the most. She was gentle, kind, loving, forgiving, patient, knowledgeable of the Word, full of the wisdom of God, compassionate, and a prayer warrior. Betsy embodied all the fruits of the Spirit found in Galatians 5:22–23a (King James Version):

> But the fruit of the Spirit is love, joy, peace, longsuffering, gentleness, goodness, faith, Meekness, temperance.

Ms. Betsy would always tell me to spend a lot of time in my "secret place." At the time I really didn't understand those words. Now I know what it is to find that special place where you meet with God and pray. She would always say, "Let Jesus love on you, honey." I couldn't sit very long, but I began to do it in obedience. Now my favorite pastime is to sit in the presence of the Lord and hear His heart's cry for His children.

I will forever be indebted and grateful for my spiritual mom, Betsy Hutcheson. She is my dear angel in disguise. I cannot express in words how awe-inspiring Ms. Betsy became to me and how God used her to begin my journey with Him.

Even though I thought very highly of Ms. Betsy, in no way did I put my trust in her. She did not allow that. She taught me instead to trust Jesus. I thank Jesus daily for being my Savior and Lord. I came to believe there was nothing impossible for God.

At this time Aglow International's mission was to lead women to Jesus Christ, to provide opportunities for Christian women to grow in their faith and to minister to others. Today, their mission statement is to carry the truth of the Kingdom that:

- Restores people to a radiant place of relationship with God and one another
- Breaks the tyranny of oppression
- Brings freedom and empowerment

As I became a part of this ministry, I was filled with the Holy Spirit and began a fresh walk with God. I was forever changed. I want to thank Aglow for helping me to understand a more excellent way in the Lord.

I would like to give honor to Aglow International (Aglow.org), especially the East Texas Area leadership team: Judy Parks, vice-president of Lighthouse Development; Lydia McCroskey, vice-president of Administration; Carol Torrance, US regional director South Central Region; Penny Montgomery, state prayer coordinator; Betsy Hutcheson, finance secretary; Ginger Giessow, public relations secretary; Barbara Watson; Liz Hardin; Oline Pond; Janet Kirk; and Jackie King.

CHAPTER 14

MEADOWLARK LEMON CAMP

Ms. Betsy and the East Texas Area Board asked me to pray and get a vision for Hemphill Aglow. I personally thought these ladies were somewhat crazy. I thought, *A vision! What was a vision?*

They explained to me, as president of the Hemphill Aglow, if I would pray, God would tell me what to do for an outreach platform for our community. I went right to work, praying for days and weeks before I got a direction.

I felt God spoke to me to do a basketball camp with Meadowlark Lemon. Meadowlark Lemon was a Christian minister. He was also well known as the celebrity "Prince Clown" for the Harlem Globetrotters. The Harlem Globetrotters were a highly sought after, world-renowned, exhibition basketball team. In their exhibitions, they showed off their basketball skills through their athleticism and their theatrical and comedy routines.

I actually started laughing. "Right! God, you want me to call this famous man and have him come to Hemphill, Texas?" My mind started racing. "How much money would this cost? Where does he live, and *why* would he want to come to Hemphill, of all places?"

I wondered how this was going to fly with our local board of Aglow since God is telling me to reach out to the youth in our community. After all, Aglow is all about reaching *women!*

I pushed all thoughts of doubt out of my mind and eagerly went to the board and conveyed my vision. When I did, some of the women were not sure about the decision I had made. I could tell some thought I missed God.

Even though the ladies had some reservations about the vision God had put on my heart, they were willing to let me do what I felt the Lord has said to do.

Wow! I was excited at the prospect of having this world-famous basketball player come to our town because I knew everything about this sport. I had played it all my life, and I still play to this day for exercise.

Basketball was my survival in my younger days. As a young girl, I ate and slept basketball. I played basketball in Jr. High at both Watauga Jr High and Smithfield Jr. High. I also went on to play in high school at North Richland Hills near Fort Worth, Texas. My senior year I was voted most valuable player and received a trophy that remained at the school. So I knew personally how much young people enjoyed this game.

My biggest challenge was to locate Meadowlark Lemon. I remember Word of Truth Family Church in Many, Louisiana, had hosted the Harlem Globetrotters. I had taken my oldest son to watch the Globetrotters and, of course, Meadowlark Lemon.

Rob, my son, wasn't as excited as I was to attend the Globetrotter's event. I didn't know at the time what God had planned for me. God had put me in the right place that night, yet it was years later when I was assigned to get in touch with Meadowlark.

With great excitement and in obedience to God's orders, I called Word of Truth Family Church to talk to Pastor Frank. I told him who I was and who I was looking for. He immediately gave me Meadowlark Lemon's contact number. I called and asked his secretary if I could talk to Meadowlark. She was gracious and kind. I went on to explain that I was president of the Hemphill Chapter of Aglow International, and I wanted to do an outreach program for the kids in our community, maybe a basketball camp. At that time, I wasn't sure if they even did basketball camps.

When Meadowlark came to the phone, I nervously told him how I had been in prayer asking God for His vision for our community. Then I pressed to ask him about a basketball camp.

I could hear the excitement in his voice. He said that he had also been in prayer concerning basketball camps. He asked God that if he was supposed to hold these camps, he wanted people to call him. After our conversation, he agreed to come.

Of course, he had a set fee for coming, which I gladly accepted. Then he gave me two options. He would come for a one-day camp, and we would pay all his expenses, plane tickets, rooms, and food for himself and Coach John Mayberry. The second option was a three-day camp, and he would pay all his and Coach Mayberry's expenses.

Well, I jumped on that like a duck on a June bug and, of course, chose the three-day camp. I immediately ran to my Aglow board members. I was so full of faith and excited over the possibilities of this God-given plan. My enthusiasm was contagious. The board couldn't help but catch the vision.

When Meadowlark arrived in Hemphill, we went to a restaurant to have breakfast. We had a very nice chat about our upcoming endeavor. He then asked me if I could have anything I wanted before camp, what would it be?

I told him about the impoverished boys and girls who would be hanging around the gym next to the location where the camp was going to be held. I knew they would want to participate in the camp but did not have the money. I would love to see them participate.

He smiled and said, "Okay, I will sponsor twenty kids." My great basketball champion was paying $2,700 so the underprivileged kids could attend the camp. I started crying and thought about the scripture that says ask and it shall be given to you.

> Ask, and it shall be given you. (Matthew 7:7a, King James Version)

The people in our community began to sponsor their own child to go. Then they felt compelled to sponsor another child as well. It started like wildfire and lit up the whole town. I was running like the Road Runner racing against Wile E. Coyote. I ran as fast as I could to collect money from everywhere. I discovered our community loved their youth and wanted to see this event go over *big*! They rocked with support!

One of my son's closest friends wasn't going to get to go to the camp because his father disapproved. Meadowlark was a black man, and in his mind, Meadowlark was just out to get rich.

Every time I approached the boy's father, he repeated the same story. "He is a black man who just wants to get rich, and I will not be supporting that." I was up against a wall. I didn't want the boy to miss out.

The boy's father was a prominent person in the county and a Christian. I could not believe he felt this way. God showed me that he was prejudiced. So I decided I would just pray for him and let God change his heart. A couple of days before the camp, I received a phone call from the man's wife. She said her husband wanted to talk to me, and would I please stop by his office.

This time, as we met at his office, he told me that God woke him up from a dream and showed him that he was prejudiced and he needed to send his son to the camp. Not only did God tell him to send his son to the camp, he also told him to pay for two African-American boys' fees as well. He wrote me a check right then and there and paid for all three boys.

Prayer changed things.

We lacked nothing. God did a mighty exploit through our local Aglow. We were a bunch of hard workers, and the fields were ripe for harvesting. We were a team that would not be denied. We had 140 kids going to the camp with about 85 percent attending free of charge.

Meadowlark was very impressed in how well the camp ran. I can hear him now, "What have you done to make this such a success?"

I told him to follow me. We had intercessory prayer going on in the locker room all day long. The intercessors were praying for the children, coaches, workers, and parents.

At the end, Meadowlark's fees were paid in full. He gave back 40 percent in tithes to our fellowship to keep us moving forward in powerful outreaches for our community.

Not only was it a fun event, it was a spiritual camp as well. Coach John Mayberry was equally as awesome with his skills and leadership ability. Seeds were planted in those young lives. Someone else will water those seeds, and God will create the increase.

It was a great blessing to have Meadowlark Lemon in our community and personally in my home. I will never forget this special time in my life.

Participants of Basketball Camp

Meadowlark Lemon and Me-Affectionately
Nicknamed "Mutt and Jeff"

MEADOWLARK LEMON MINISTRIES, INC.

"A merry heart doeth good like a medicine..." Proverbs 17:22

13610 N. Scottsdale Rd.
Suite 10267
Scottsdale, AZ 85254
Phone: 602 / 951-0030
Fax: 602 / 951-3757
e-mail:
meadowlarklemon@inficad.com

Meadowlark Lemon Ministries Outreaches:

The Meadowlark Lemon T.V. Show
Evangelical Outreach
Camp Meadowlark
Youth Outreach
Basketball Camps and Clinics
Vacation Bible School
Youth Prisons
Ministry to Athletes
Health and Fitness
Hospital Visitation
Youth Drug Awareness Program
Ministry to Native Americans

March 25, 1998

Jeanette Golden
Hemphill Aglow Fellowship
P.O. Box 100
Hemphill, TX 75948

Dear Jeanette,

On behalf of our entire staff, I would like to thank you for doing such a wonderful job of conducting Camp Meadowlark in the Hemphill area. The camp as well as the outreach service was a success. Special thanks to you and your committee for making it happen. They both allowed me to participant in one of my life time pleasures of meeting people.

I am thankful every day that I have been given the unique opportunity to intermingle with a wide variety of people from all walks of life. My past has been used to open the door for many individuals' futures. My life as a basketball celebrity was no accident and because of it, I have access to millions. These are millions who might not otherwise hear the good news message that burns within me. I know that this is a gift and like all gifts of value, I do cherish it.

Once again thank you and I pray the best for you and the wonderful things that you are doing within the Community of Hemphill, Texas.

Joyfully,

Meadowlark

Personal Note from Meadowlark Lemon

CHAPTER 15

BETHLEHEM LIVE

Working with Aglow, I learned the value of fasting and praying. It didn't take me long to understand the meaning of "Get a vision." I was filled with faith and anxious to get a new word from God. Therefore, without hesitation, I asked Him for my next assignment: "What should we do next to bring more of Your light to our community?"

In the meantime, God brought a wonderful lady into my life named Lisa Ison. Lisa was from Georgia and had a musical ministry called Three Women. I invited her to Hemphill to bring her spiritual and moving performance to our city.

We held the musical in town at the Junior Huffman Public Theater. She did an anointed rendering of dramatic roles in music, songs, and dance. It was a great success, and the community loved it.

The performance changed some lives forever as they met Jesus for the first time. They invited Him to reside in their heart.

Lisa and I stayed in touch, and one day she asked me if I had ever done a Christmas musical. I just had to chuckle because I am not musically inclined at all. I certainly couldn't orchestrate a musical.

I agreed to pray about it. One day, while in prayer, the Lord said to me, "*Bethlehem Live.*" I knew this certainly was from God, so I ran with the vision. I never dreamed this would come near to being a Hollywood production.

Later, Lisa and I got together to discuss the *Bethlehem Live* musical. She was just as excited as I was. Our enthusiasm began to build as she began to share what would be needed to do to prepare for the production.

We would have to replicate the city of Bethlehem and make costumes. We would have to produce live animals, provide food for them and people to attend to them. I suddenly had a reality check. I thought, *Hold on, girl, you don't own a zoo!*

Lisa kept talking, and in my mind I was calculating dollar signs. I was beginning to get cold feet as my head was full of questions: *Where will the money come from to purchase these many things? Where do you get live animals, food to feed and skilled caretakers? Are the women on the board of Aglow willing to take on such a mega task?*

Lisa said, "We need material for costumes. There will be 110 cast members."

I questioned, "Costumes for 110 cast members? That's a lot of material."

Lisa smiled and said, "Yes, it is, so let's go fabric shopping."

As we got in the car, I was thinking, *God, I hope your checkbook is big enough to cover all of these expenses!*

We went to the fabric store and asked to speak to the owner. We shared with him about our show, *Bethlehem Live*. A miracle happened right before our eyes!

The owner responded, "Pick out all the fabric you need. You will only pay $40 to pay for shipping the fabric and supplies to your home."

God answered my question, "Yes, Jeanette, I have a big checkbook."

The community was also excited about the live musical. They volunteered to help in any way they could. Most of the churches in Hemphill got involved, as well as churches from out of town.

First Baptist Church in North Richland Hills in Fort Worth, where my family attended, cut out all the patterns for our costumes. Then we had the women in Hemphill who knew how to sew pitch in with their talents.

Other eager volunteers carved out shepherd's staffs. A local lumber company donated all the lumber to build the needed structures. Gary and I built our version of the city of Bethlehem. Paint was donated by a paint store in Shreveport, Louisiana. The school art class painted the city.

People from Hemphill furnished the animals and took care of them. We also brought in singers and dancers. Most of the businesses, organizations, and individuals in our fair city either donated money, materials, or their time.

The stage was set, scenes were written, the singers, dancers and actors were chosen, all the finishing details had been completed, and after dozens and dozens of rehearsals, we were ready for opening night. God had taken the faith of a mustard seed and grown *Bethlehem Live* into a huge oak tree. The show was a huge success.

We did this production about three or four years. We had an average of four hundred people in attendance each evening. We wanted our community to know the true meaning of Christmas and the birth of our Lord and Savior, Jesus Christ. Many souls were born again in our little town of Bethlehem.

Cast Members

CHAPTER 16

BREAKING BREAD YOUTH CENTER

Hemphill, Texas, was a small town, yet we had a great group of young people. The Lord spoke to Gary and me to open a youth center. We felt our teenagers should have a place to congregate and enjoy wholesome activities.

After some searching, we came upon a vacant building in town called the Old Boat Place. We rented it for $750 per month. We decided to call the center the Breaking Bread Youth Center. We wanted it to be exactly that, a place where young people could break bread together and also be fed the bread of life, Jesus.

Our sons, Rob, Kurt, and Drew, got on board with the project and cleaned out all the debris in the building. It seemed like they carried out enough bricks to build a house. They swept down all the cobwebs and swept out all the bugs that had called this place home.

After the deep cleaning, other young people came in with paint cans and paint brushes. They were very talented and used their skills to decorate the walls with their unique artwork. They drew biblical masterpieces and added hand-painted scriptures. When finished, their creativity provided a colorful, peaceful, and welcoming location for all to enjoy.

We rented pool tables and other game tables for the young people's entertainment. We also served cold drinks and food to eat. The Breaking Bread Youth Center was open Thursday through Saturday from 7:00 p.m. to 12:00 p.m.

We brought in Christian bands that provided some truly tremendous praise and worship music. There were also Bible teachings catered to the needs of the youth.

It was an awesome sight to watch the happy teens come and go. They would sit and talk or play their guitars, laughing and cutting up. Great friendships were formed, and hearts were bonded.

As with many small towns, there was little for the youth to do and no place to go. The youth center served as a safe haven for many of the youth in our community. And of course, it helped to keep them off the streets and out of trouble.

The Breaking Bread Youth Center was a great success, and God changed the lives of many of our Hemphill youth. Some that had gotten derailed got back on track.

After a period of time, a terrible storm blew through our town and took the building with it. Of course, we were all saddened but felt the center had served its purpose. Thank you, Lord!

My Three Sons and Their Friends

CHAPTER 17

RESTORATION OF FAMILY

I was working for West Sabine Independent School District as an elementary physical education teacher. One day, while at work, I was checking my daily emails. I was confused to have received a communication from a woman by the name of Dakota Idell. You could have knocked me over with a feather when I read the following words, "Are you my Aunt, and if you are, would you please contact me?"

I was very nervous about this email because I had not heard from anyone in my biological family for thirty-eight years. I did not respond right away. I shared the email with my husband and my adoptive sister, Terri. We prayed about it at the time. We agreed to continue to pray until we heard from the Lord to get His clear direction in the matter. Several weeks went by.

One day as I was seeking the Lord, He reminded me that I had prayed concerning my family many, many years ago. I had told God that if He ever wanted me to make a connection with my family, they would have to contact me.

Obviously, someone had contacted me. I pondered over the name Dakota Idell. I knew my oldest sister had married a man by the name Ethan Idell. They had a daughter named Dakota Idell.

I decided to answer the email because I had a lot of questions. I first asked Dakota, "What was your mother's name?"

She answered, "Abbigail Grace Jones Idell."

Chills ran down my spine. I knew that was my sister's full given name.

I next asked, "What was your dad's name?"

She answered, "Ethan Idell."

Again, I was chilled to the bone. I knew that Ethan Idell was my brother-in-law.

My hands shook as I typed, "Who is your grandmother?"

She answered, "Falicia Maud Tweedy."

That was definitely my mom's name.

I continued, "Do you have any pictures of your family?"

"Yes," she said, and "I will send some to you by email."

When the pictures came through, I saw a picture of my mom and my uncle in an embrace. I thought to myself, *Where is my aunt Monna?* Monna was my mom's sister. She was the sweetest woman you would ever meet. I thought, *Did my mom take my aunt's husband away from her?*

I once again quizzed Dakota. I asked, "Where is Aunt Monna?"

It saddened me to hear, "Aunt Monna died." There was no doubt in my mind that this was my family. Now I had to make another decision. Was I going to let them back into my life?

Again, I went to my prayer closet, and after giving it some serious thought, I knew in my heart I wanted the relationship with my family to be restored. I had forgiven my mom many years ago, but it was going to take a heart of love to meet, hold, and touch my mom. I definitely needed the fruit of the Spirit of God's divine love.

> But the fruit of the Spirit is love, joy, peace, longsuffering, gentleness, goodness, faith, Meekness, temperance. (Galatians 5:22–23a, King James Version)

After making man, Adam, and his counterpart, Eve, one of the first commandments God gave them was to be fruitful and multiply. In God's divine blueprint, He planned for man to have a family, a love relationship.

Family bonds are God-breathed and God-ordained. When this bond is disrupted for whatever reason there is an instinctive longing for that love relationship to be restored. Even though I was ready for the reconciliation with my biological family, I had a huge hurdle in my path.

My adoptive mom was battling a fatal lung disease. I would never do anything to disrespect her. Mom Barbara gave generously when it came to her time, resources, and most of all, her love. She taught me how to love God, my husband, and my children with my whole heart.

At this crucial time, Mom Barbara was in severe pain, and I did not want to worsen that pain or worry her by bringing up the situation with my biological family. I knew, however, she would be the one person I could go to for counsel. I knew she would be able to guide me with godly wisdom, knowledge, and understanding.

My adoptive mom was and still is the person I consider to be my real mom. She is the mother who taught me how to love and how to forgive. I had to decide. Would I be deceiving her if I held back the truth of what was going on with my biological family?

I was also concerned that she might not be able to handle the news with all the physical situations she was facing. Lastly, I considered what she would have done if she were in my shoes. After much prayer, I decided to tell her what was going on.

I told her that my biological mother had made contact with me and I needed her honest opinion. Should I allow this woman back into my life? I knew I personally wanted to, but I am telling you, I would have honored Mom Barb's last words on the matter if she had said no. Thank God she said, "Jeanette, that's a decision between you, God, and Gary."

I chose to go to Tennessee to see my family. I must admit, it was somewhat difficult to do, but I had forgiven everyone, including my stepfather, the devil himself. Yet if my mom would have still been with him, she would never have come back into my life. I stayed in Tennessee for a week. It was good visit but awkward. My mom was not living in a very safe place in Memphis.

That summer Gary and the boys went to Tennessee to meet their mother-in-law and grandmother for the first time in their lives. They also met the extended family, uncles, aunts, etc.

My adoptive mom was in ICU and not going to make it. My biological mother was consoling me over the phone from her home in Tennessee. That was a very strange feeling, and I never really understood it, but I knew God was doing a restoration work between me and my mom.

As I witnessed my adoptive mom, whom I had loved and adored, slip into eternity, I was moved to tears as my biological mother tried to comfort me. I had never felt the compassion she now extended toward me. With my stepfather out of the picture, she was free to extend love toward me the way she had always wanted to but didn't know how.

In the Bible, Genesis 37 gives an account of a portion of the life of Joseph. I feel that my life compares somewhat with Joseph. Joseph was thrown into a pit and sold into slavery by his brothers out of jealousy, hatred, and envy.

When I was young and living at home with my biological mother and stepfather, I felt betrayed by my mother. I had become a slave to my stepfather's abuse and my mother's neglect to save me from this horrible situation. I felt I had been thrown into a pit of despair with no way of escape.

As a child, I did not understand why my mother did not come to the aid of my sister and me. As an adult, I can see now that she was so afraid of my stepfather, she was frozen in fear. I am sure she too felt like a prisoner, steeping in low self-esteem and finally succumbing to deep depression and a sense of unworthiness. I imagine that my mother was blanketed with feelings of shame and self-hatred because of not coming to our aid.

In Egypt, Joseph was promoted to a position of high authority. God had taken him from the pit to the palace.

There was a famine in Canaan where Joseph's father and brothers lived. Joseph's brothers were sent to Egypt by their father to get food. When Joseph saw his brothers, God melted his heart to receive them with love. Genesis 45 says that Joseph forgave his brothers, and they wept in each other's embrace. God miraculously restored their relationship.

Genesis 50:20 (King James Version) reads,

> But as for you, ye thought evil against me;
> but God meant it unto good.

In Hebrew the word meant means "fabricate." So God fabricated something good out of what Joseph's brothers meant for evil. This, of course, was a plot entirely orchestrated by Satan.

I felt I, too, had gone from the pit to the palace. God saved me from the situation I was in. I was adopted into a loving Christian family. I married a godly man, a doctor who was making a good living. I had been healed miraculously and had given birth to three wonderful sons. I became president of the Aglow and watched as God used our organization in a mighty way to reach out to our little town in Christian love.

What the enemy had meant for my destruction God had manufactured for good. To put the icing on the cake, God restored my relationship with my biological family.

My biological mom moved to Hemphill, and we started a fresh, new relationship. She started going to church with me. After our many years apart, I am very pleased to know that my mother has a personal and intimate relationship with our Heavenly Father and His precious Son, Jesus.

My Biological Mother and Me

CHAPTER 18

A Force to Be Reckoned With

Gary and I had become local pastors at Word of Truth Family Church in Hemphill, Texas. One day a couple came to us with a project they felt God wanted them to do. They had purchased a large sign of the Ten Commandments as written in Exodus 20. At the bottom of the sign, it read, "With God All Things Are Possible." Our church prayed about it and decided this would be a great way to display God's written word.

Gary and I owned some land on Highway 21 near Pendleton Harbor. We began construction of a frame for the sign. It was finished in August 2013. The community seemed to love the sign, and we were receiving compliments from everyone.

Guess what happened next? On November 20, 2013, a complaint was filed by a local resident who was offended by the sign. In February 2014, I received a removal notice from TXDOT (Texas Department of Transportation) that my sign was noncompliant with TXDOT rules for outdoor advertising. TXDOT ordered me to remove my Ten Commandments sign within forty-five days.

Wanting to protect my freedom of speech and defend my religious liberty, I contacted TXDOT to find out what I needed to do to keep my sign displayed. TXDOT informed me that I needed to obtain an outdoor advertising permit, a minimum $2,500 surety bond, and an outdoor advertising license. TXDOT also threatened that if I failed to comply with their requirements, it could result in fines of $500 to $1,000 per day.

I decided to take some time to consider my options. I then considered the substantial time and money it would take to satisfy TXDOT's requirements. However, before I could apply for an outdoor advertising license, I received a letter from TXDOT's associate general counsel stating that my sign was located near a road that was statutorily prohibited from having signage at all and thus my sign could not be permitted. In other words, TXDOT instituted an outright ban on all noncommercial signs along the road adjacent to my property. Commercial signs, however, were permitted.

I did not much like this proclamation, so I decided to be a force to be reckoned with.

Mathew 19:26 (King James Version) reads,

> But Jesus looked at them and said to them, "With men this is impossible, but with God all things are possible."

My road sign stated this very verse. I prayed about it and decided I would step out on faith and act on God's Word that all things are possible with Him.

I called KTRE Television station, Channel 9, in Lufkin, Texas. A news reporter by the name of Donna McCollum talked with me. She agreed that my story needed to be told. She immediately set up a time for an on-site interview. I barely had time to draw my community together. With the short time frame, I was only able to get around forty people to meet at the sign for the television broadcast.

Reporter Donna McCollum and her crew aired the story, and immediately, Facebook and Twitter went absolutely wild. Everyone was supporting our rights to post the sign.

To paraphrase 2 Kings 6:16: "There were more *for us* than there were *against us*" (emphasis mine).

KTRE wanted to run another story. I was elated that we were getting the coverage we needed to fight this battle.

The community rallied. We opened a bank account to take donations to have Ten Commandment car magnets and yard signs made. Businesses displayed the signs in their work places. We made T-shirts and wore them in our community to stand up for our freedom of speech and religious faith.

It seemed like the whole community got behind us. What began as a spark soon turned into a wildfire. I had people calling from everywhere wanting to do a story. Even New York Times Magazine online called.

Other towns like Carthage, Texas, Henderson, Texas, Houston, Texas, Marshall, Texas, Memphis, Tennessee, cities in California, as well as other cities in other states, began putting signs up and in their cars and on their property.

This went on for months before Liberty Institute called to see if they could legally represent me. Liberty Institute's senior counsel Mike Berry came to Hemphill. After some discussion, I signed a contract agreeing to their terms to represent me in a legal suit.

That was one of the best days of my life. I didn't have to answer any more phone calls from news people. All I had to do was direct them to Mike Berry. He was truly awesome in his support and carried through on the project.

Liberty Institute immediately sent a letter to TXDOT. They stated that the forced removal of Mrs. Golden's sign from her private property violated both federal and state religious liberty and freedom of speech laws. This included the Texas Religious Freedom Restoration Act (TRFRA), the Federal Religious Land Use and Institutionalized Persons Act (RLUIPA), the US Constitution, and the Texas Constitution. Liberty Institute requested that TXDOT rescind its removal order and allow Mrs. Golden to maintain her sign without the requirement of a license, bond, or permit.

At that time, Liberty Institute senior counsel Mike Berry said in a statement, "It is outrageous that TXDOT is preventing Texans from having signs on their own private property. Religious freedom and private property rights are some of the most sacred rights Texans and Americans enjoy dating back to the founding of Texas and our nation."

TXDOT responded positively to Liberty Institute's demand, acknowledging that its rule was likely unlawful. In response, TXDOT agreed to revise its rules regarding non-commercial signage on private property to protect individual's rights to freedom of speech. They further stated, once the new rule becomes final, "Texans like Mrs. Golden will be allowed to freely express their religious beliefs on their private property."

Liberty Institute applauded TXDOT's cooperation and their commitment to amending Department of Transportation rules to reflect respect for a citizen's most sacred constitutional freedoms of religious freedom and private property rights. Counsel Mike Berry commended the ruling "as a win that will benefit all Texans who value liberty."

Prior to the rule change, only commercial signs were allowed with a license, bond, and permit. But with the change in policy, signs that did not exceed 96 square feet in size, sit on private property, and did not promote a business are exempt from the license, bond and permit requirements. TXDOT stated that my Ten Commandments sign was 72 square feet in size and therefore satisfied the exemption criteria.

In TXDOT's letter to me announcing the new exemption, Associate General Ronald M. Johnson said, "I personally would like to thank you and Liberty Institute for bringing this issue to our attention. The rights of the citizens of Texas are better protected today because of all our efforts. This has been a civics lesson in how democratic government is supposed to work and it would not have happened without you."

After all was said and done, I feel TXDOT did the right thing, and I am forever grateful for all their efforts above and beyond cooperation.

I always believed in my heart there would be a change in the rules that would allow me to keep my sign, as well as other Texans wanting to express their religious views on their property. As it states on my sign, "WITH GOD ALL THINGS ARE POSSSIBLE."

When victory was won, I kept reading this scripture reference over and over:

> WITH GOD ALL THINGS ARE POSSIBLE.

Liberty Institute, on behalf of client Jeanette Golden of Hemphill, Texas, and the Texas Department of Transportation (TXDOT) jointly announced an official change to TXDOT's rules and regulations regarding private speech on private property.

God changed the law in the state of Texas for the Ten Commandments sign to stay in its place. Until this day, the community still has signs up all over the county. Businesses display the signs in their stores, and people still have the magnets on their cars.

I would like to acknowledge the ministry of Philip and Suzy Klevmoen in Kalispell, Montana. They make signs and banners, and their goal is to canvas the world with the Word of God. It was through this connection that we purchased our Ten Commandments sign. If you would like more information, their website is Gods10.com, and Philip's email address is pkmail@earthlink.net. His phone number is (702) 271-9288.

I would like to acknowledge Texas State Senator Robert Nichols: District 3. Senator Nichols serves as chairman of the Senate Transportation Committee. During his six sessions as a state senator, Robert Nichols authored and passed Legislation to protect landowner's rights. He played an important role in my battle over the Ten Commandment sign.

Pictured (left to right) Dr. Gary Golden, Jeanette Golden and Pastor Frank Ebarb

Jeanette Golden Case

One Texan's stand for religious freedom results in change in the law

In February 2014, the Texas Department of Transportation (TXDOT) ordered Jeanette Golden to remove a Ten Commandments sign she had placed on her private property near Hemphill, Texas. TXDOT stated her sign was noncompliant with requirements for "outdoor advertising" and later stated that signs were completely prohibited on her property that is adjacent to a state highway. In May 2014, First Liberty sent a demand letter to TXDOT on Mrs. Golden's behalf, and in September 2014, First Liberty and TXDOT jointly announced a rule change that allowed Mrs. Golden to keep her sign conveying a religious message.

Liberty Institute's Web Post of Case Won

CHAPTER 19

THE BRUSH OF ANGELS

On the many occasions when I am asked if I believe in angels, I wonder how anyone could doubt their existence. I am always reminded of Mom Barbara sitting in an old rocking chair, slowly rocking back and forth with that big black book, the Bible, in her lap.

My siblings and I listened intently as she read aloud to us about God and His angels. She taught us that each individual is assigned their very own guardian angel to protect us from harm as well as to dissuade us from harming others.

She said there are two kingdoms in the world, the kingdom of light and the kingdom of darkness. The kingdom of light is the kingdom of God and His angelic beings. The kingdom of darkness is ruled by Satan and his demons.

Since God made each of us to be a free moral agent, there are choices in life that we must make. We can choose life or death, blessings or curses, good or evil. What we choose most definitely affects our future and the future of anyone who is directly or indirectly influenced by our decisions.

I know that angels have been posted with me throughout my life to give me instruction, guidance and protection.

Psalm 91:11 (King James Version) reads,

> For He shall give His angels charge over
> thee, to keep thee in all thy ways.

I have a new life now. I have the peaceful bliss of knowing that I am an overcomer and not a victim. The life I left behind does not define me. However, removing me from my past was exceedingly difficult. It was not without effort. I climbed out of traps that were strategically placed in my path by the enemy. I was forced to make the painful decision to leave my biological family behind. I left some of them for a season, and some for a lifetime.

I no longer wake up from horrifying nightmares. I no longer long for a teddy bear or doll for comfort. God has gifted me with a godly husband to snuggle up to at night and to share my life with. Gary, my true love, has filled every part of my life with hope and joy. And through the years, his encouragement and support have helped me to be an overcomer.

Since the day we met, Gary and I have been painting on our canvas of life together. When the painting was completed, I took a step back and saw that some strokes of the brush were beautiful while others were very ugly. There were splashes of color from Gary's life and splashes from mine. As I looked closely, it was easy for me to see that the most beautiful strokes on the canvas were the ones we had made together. We had created a masterpiece in our three sons. Gary graciously touched my life like the beautiful, indelible colors on a fine oil painting.

When I look at the canvas of my life, I also see the unmistakable brush of God's angels.

Yes, I do believe in angels!

CHAPTER 20

The Oak Tree

I love nature, and I love spending time outside. It is so relaxing to sit under a large oak tree and enjoy the atmosphere and the surroundings.

I sit in silence, looking up into the sky, and often observe the constantly changing cloud formations. I think about the various objects the moving clouds resemble. I listen to the singing of the birds and watch them fly over. I was hoping they would not leave their signature of tiny white snow droppings in my hair.

I study the oak tree and wondered how old it is. How far does its roots extend underground? While its leaves move gently in the breeze, I contemplate on the significance of the tree.

An oak tree is one of the strongest, sturdiest, and longest-living trees in the world. Its leaves are countless, and it becomes ever more beautiful as it ages. Its roots grow deep within the earth where they seek out moisture to sustain its life through drought conditions. These roots provide a firm anchor so that neither high winds nor torrential rains will take it down. The durability of this tree has set it apart from all the others.

Just like every other living thing, the oak tree goes through stages of growth. It begins life as a simple seed, an acorn planted deep within the soil. With time, it grows into a magnificent, indescribably strong ecosystem wherein other creatures find refuge from predators, shade from scorching heat, shelter from winter storms, and a haven from rushing floodwaters.

Ironically, the very tree that began as a helpless seed is now a resource for helpless creatures. Animals instinctively know that the oak tree is a safe place. Somehow, they sense that it can withstand the earth's ravages. It has survived life's calms and life's chaos. It is in the oak tree's DNA to be what it is, strong.

The symbolism of the oak tree goes deeper than something tangible we can touch and or something beautiful to the eye. It goes deeper than simply a place to find shade or shelter. Although its beginning was fragile and uncertain, its branches now point upward as if to give God reverence for what He has created.

We have all suffered and endured the elements of life. We have weathered storms and survived desert-like droughts. We have certainly experienced growing pains at one time or another. What we may not have realized at those times of uncertainly is that, if you have put your trust in God, a seed has been planted within our hearts. If you are grounded in Him, the challenges you face along the way will only make you stronger. It is within our DNA to overcome.

The weight of this life will try to pull us down. But if our faith is directed upward, like the oak tree, we will mature and become a useful instrument for God to use.

Having overcome many challenges in my own life, I want to be like the oak, a survivor. I want to be a provider of refuge to those who need comfort and understanding.

I know that not everyone will understand my world, yet I am at peace with the road I have traveled. I am not ashamed of who I am because I know that God made me, and because He is good, I am good. God does not make junk.

Like the oak tree, my roots are grounded, grounded in Him Who created me. The Maker Who planned the strength of the oak tree as well as its uses and abilities is also the very one Who gave me the ability to be strong in Him. I will continue to look upward in the direction I was intended to reach.

I know God planned my life before the foundation of the world and like the oak tree I have DNA. God, in His infinite wisdom, took my DNA and carefully and very deliberately spelled out, *Jeanette Jones Golden.*

CHAPTER 21

THE WARRIOR INSIDE

I suppose I have always been a fighter. As a young girl, I could whip any boy. I was strong physically. I believe God made me that way knowing I would have to fight many battles to become the overcomer and spiritual warrior that I am today.

I have fought my way through sexual abuse and an immoral lifestyle patterned by my biological family. Becoming homeless left me with a feeling of worthlessness, anxiety, fear, and depression.

When I think back to my youth when my older sister approached me, forewarning me of the sexual abuse I was bound to face, she handed me a weapon. It was the only weapon I had—a tiny safety pin! Even though I used all the force that I had as a young girl to thwart off the attacks of my stepfather with my safety pin, it was to no avail. That little weapon proved to be of no use to me.

I give all thanks and praise to God from delivering me from the trials and sufferings of my early years. I have walked a long and rocky road to be where I am today. I am no longer a child, equipped with a useless little safety pin to defend myself. I have been taught and trained to know who I am in the Lord Jesus Christ. I have learned that I have been given weapons of warfare to defend myself in the battles of life. I have learned my only true enemy is Satan and his demonic forces. That is why we must put on the whole armor of God.

Ephesians 6:10–18 (King James Version) reads,

> Finally, my brethren, be strong in the Lord, and in the power of his might.
>
> Put on the whole armor of God, that ye may be able to stand against the wiles of the devil.
>
> For we wrestle not against flesh and blood, but against principalities, against powers, against the rulers of the darkness of this world, against spiritual wickedness in high places.
>
> Wherefore take unto you the whole armor of God, that ye may be able to withstand in the evil day, and having done all, to stand.
>
> Stand therefore, having your loins girt about with truth, and having on the breastplate of righteousness;
>
> And your feet shod with the preparation of the gospel of peace;

> Above all, taking the shield of faith, wherewith ye shall be able to quench all the fiery darts of the wicked.
>
> And take the helmet of salvation, and the sword of the Spirit, which is the word of God:
>
> Praying always with all prayer and supplication in the Spirit, and watching thereunto with all perseverance and supplication for all saints.

Each of these pieces of armor has a special meaning.

The *helmet of salvation* is, of course, our salvation from hell, death, and the grave. *Salvation* is an all-inclusive word. God has saved us from sickness, disease, poverty, and any other dreadful thing that should befall us.

The *breastplate of righteousness* covers us with the blood of the Lamb, Jesus Christ. We are made righteous through Him, and no weapon can penetrate the breastplate of righteousness.

The *shield of faith* is a very important piece of the armor. Our faith in God grows as we grow up in Him. It is a lifelong process of building up our faith in a true and living God.

In the Ancient East, both men and women wore long tunics, and around the tunics they wore a belt. As the men were called into battle, they would pull the tunic from behind and tuck it into the belt in front. This way they were prepared to run to the battle.

"To gird up your loins with truth" means to be prepared to run to the battle. The Bible says that Jesus is the truth, the light, and the way. We are not in this battle alone.

"To shod your feet with the gospel of peace" means to put your boots on! No good soldier would go to battle without their boots on. I read that Roman soldiers had nails protruding from the bottom of their boots, which would be like today's athletes wearing cleats on the bottom of their shoes. It gives them a firm footing as they run or walk on rough terrain.

"Praying in the Spirit" refers to praying in tongues. Praying in tongues is one of the most powerful ways to pray. As you pray in tongues, you are praying in an unknown language, known only by God. As you pray in your prayer language, you are praying the will of God.

Romans 8:26 (King James Version) reads,

> Likewise the Spirit also helpeth our infirmities: for we know not what we should pray for as we ought: but the Spirit itself maketh intercession for us with groanings which cannot be uttered.

"The sword of the Spirit" refers to the Word of God, the Bible. You see, I no longer carry a tiny little safety pin as a weapon to fight off my enemy. God has given me a sword, a huge, magnificent sword! I can use this weapon and deliver a deadly blow with the strength of God's full power.

I have always been a fighter. However, I no longer wrestle with little boys on the playground. I have come to understand that I am a warrior in the army of God.

1 Corinthians 13:11 (King James Version) reads,

> When I was a child, I spake as a child, I understood as a child, I thought as a child: but when I became a man, I put away childish things.

The phrase "a man" in this scripture is translated to mean a "person" or "human being." Therefore, you can exchange the word man for woman.

The warrior inside me has come out and shown herself to be victorious. It has certainly not been because of my own efforts or in my own strength. It is only through Jesus Christ that I am able to stand and fight.

I praise God for the warrior inside!

CHAPTER 22

JUST AS I AM

There is a well-known hymn entitled "Just As I Am." I can truly say when I received Jesus as my Lord and Savior, He received me "just as I was!" Without a doubt I carried with me wounds, scars, and sins that were deep and dark. In no way did I deserve His forgiveness.

The title of my book is *The Warrior Inside*. As I have stated, I was always a fighter. I had been taught to steal just to have food to eat. You can understand how difficult it might have been for me to understand that salvation is a gift, something free. I did not have to steal, beg, or borrow to get this free gift. I did not have to put forth any effort. I had only to believe.

Ephesians 2:8–9 (Amplified Bible) reads,

> For it is by grace [God's remarkable compassion and favor drawing you to Christ] that you have been saved [actually

> delivered from judgment and given eternal life] through faith. And this [salvation] is not of yourselves [not through your own effort], but it is the [undeserved, gracious] gift of God; not as a result of [your] works [nor your attempts to keep the Law], so that no one will [be able to] boast or take credit in any way [for his salvation].

The key phrase in this scripture is "by grace through faith." Grace is God's gift to you. Faith is a trust and confidence you have that God is true to His word. If you ask God in faith, you will receive His forgiveness.

I know some may think, "But, Jeanette, you don't know what I've done and how I have lived. It is too late for me."

> For all have sinned, and come short of the glory of God. (Romans 3:23, King James Version)

In this scripture reference the word "all" means "all." There is not a person who has not sinned. It does not matter if you are rich or poor, young or old, male or female, or the color of your skin; all have sinned.

When Jesus hung on the cross, there was a thief on either side of him. One of the thieves mocked him, but the other one asked Jesus to remember him. At the last hour, Jesus forgave this man his sins. It is never too late.

Luke 23:39–43 (Amplified Bible) reads,

> One of the criminals who had been hanged [on a cross beside Him] kept hurling abuse at Him, saying, "Are You not the Christ? Save Yourself and us [from death]!" But the other one rebuked him, saying, "Do you not even fear God, since you are under the same sentence of condemnation? We are suffering justly, because we are getting what we deserve for what we have done; but this Man has done nothing wrong." And he was saying, "Jesus, [please] remember me when You come into Your kingdom!" Jesus said to him, "I assure you and most solemnly say to you, today you will be with Me in Paradise."

The words of the thief on the cross were simple. His heartfelt cry was, "Remember me." No doubt those words pricked the heart of Jesus. His response, "Today you will be with Me in Paradise" is proof of His everlasting love toward all men.

> For God so loved the world, that he gave his only begotten Son, that whosoever believeth in him should not perish, but have everlasting life. (John 3:16, King James Version)

Romans 10:9–10 (King James Version) reads,

> That if thou shalt confess with thy mouth the Lord Jesus, and shalt believe in thine heart that God hath raised him from the dead, thou shalt be saved.
>
> For with the heart man believeth unto righteousness; and with the mouth confession is made unto salvation.

If you believe that Jesus died for your sins and you wish to receive your salvation, all you need to do is confess with your mouth and believe in your heart just as the Scripture says. If this is your desire, pray this simple prayer:

> Father, in the name of Jesus, I come to you just as I am, a sinner. I believe You died on the cross and rose from the dead so that I might have everlasting life. I ask You, in Jesus's name to come into my heart and forgive me for all my sins. I want You to be Lord and Savior of my life. I pray this in the name of Jesus Christ. Amen.

Now that you have received Jesus Christ as your personal savior, you are saved, a born again child of God!

I once lived a loveless life in a loveless family. God, in His mercy and grace, steered me down a path that led me to be adopted into a loving Christian family. As I continued down the road of life and received Jesus as my personal Savior I became part of a larger family, the family of God. I now welcome you into that same family.

CHAPTER 23

One Thing Remains—His Power

As a child I often felt abandoned, a castaway. I lay in the dark, knowing I would be faced with unspeakable torment. I lay under a bridge, isolated from the world. Those feelings of being alone and forsaken are a vague memory to me now. At the time, however, it was painful and fearful to know that I had only me, myself, and, I to count on to survive. I thank the Lord for my loving family and for having Jesus in my life.

Imagine how wonderful it must have been for the disciples, those who walked and talked with Jesus day after day while they were alive on this earth. They loved Him, and He loved them. Then one day, He told them that He must leave them. I am sure they were shocked. Their hearts' cry must have been, "No, don't go!"

At the time they did not understand why. Jesus knew they were distressed and confused. He gave them this promise:

> And I will ask the Father, and He will give you another Helper (Comforter, Advocate, Intercessor—Counselor, Strengthener, Standby), to be with you forever. (John 14:16, Amplified Bible)

Although the disciples trusted Him, they still did not fully comprehend the meaning of this statement. After the cross, Jesus's death, burial, and resurrection, He came back to the disciples for forty days before He ascended into heaven.

Before leaving for heaven's portals, Jesus gave His disciples and those who believed in Him another command and a promise.

> While being together and eating with them, He commanded them not to leave Jerusalem, but to wait for what the Father had promised, "Of which," He said, "you have heard Me speak. For John baptized with water, but you will be baptized and empowered and united with the Holy Spirit, not long from now." (Acts 1:4–5, Amplified Bible)

> But you will receive power and ability when the Holy Spirit comes upon you; and you will be My witnesses [to tell people about Me] both in Jerusalem and in all Judea, and Samaria, and even to the ends of the earth. (Acts 1:8, Amplified Bible)

On His command, they waited, they prayed, then they waited and prayed even more. There were many who followed Jesus because of the miracles, signs, and wonders He performed on earth, but only a few remained in the Upper Room, where they had gathered to pray. Jesus was faithful to keep His word.

> When the day of Pentecost had come, they were all together in one place, and suddenly a sound came from heaven like a rushing violent wind, and it filled the whole house where they were sitting. There appeared to them tongues resembling fire, which were being distributed [among them], and they rested on each one of them [as each person received the Holy Spirit]. And they were all filled [that is, diffused throughout their being] with the Holy Spirit and began to speak in other tongues (different languages), as the Spirit was giving them the ability to speak out [clearly and appropriately]. (Acts 2:1–4, Amplified Bible)

As I have said before, I was taught the experience of receiving the Holy Spirit with the evidence of speaking in other tongues or languages was no longer relevant to the church today. I guess a lot of people have figured we can do it all by ourselves!

There are many scriptures in the New Testament that speak of the experience of being baptized with the Holy Spirit and the importance of it.

John the Baptist spoke these words:

> I indeed have baptized you with water: but he shall baptize you with the Holy Ghost. (Mark 1:8, King James Version)

> Then Peter said unto them, Repent, and be baptized every one of you in the name of Jesus Christ for the remission of sins, and ye shall receive the gift of the Holy Ghost.
>
> For the promise is unto you, and to your children, and to all that are afar off, even as many as the LORD our God shall call. (Acts 2:38–39, King James Version)

> For one who speaks in an unknown tongue does not speak to people but to God; for no one understands him or catches his meaning, but by the Spirit he speaks mysteries [secret truths, hidden things]. (1 Corinthians 4:2)

The apostle Paul spoke of the Baptism of the Holy Spirit.

> What is it then? I will pray with the spirit, and I will pray with the understanding

> also: I will sing with the spirit, and I will sing with the understanding also." (1 Corinthians 14:15, King James Version)
>
> But ye, beloved, building up yourselves on your most holy faith, praying in the Holy Ghost. (Jude 1:20, King James Version)

The New Testaments saints received the Baptism and multitudes after them. There have been many outpourings of the Holy Spirit since Bible days, and many have received a one on one experience with God.

I want to go back to the first scripture I quoted, John 14:6. These words stand out: "Helper (Comforter, Advocate, Intercessor—Counselor, Strengthener, Standby)." There are times when you must draw from the power of God in the stormy seas of life. You can stand in the dark, but not until you flip the light switch do you have eyes to see and ears to hear. I don't know about you, but there are times when I need the Holy Spirit as my helper, comforter, advocate, intercessor, counselor, strengthener, and standby.
The Holy Spirit is Jesus's promise that He would not leave us alone or forsake us.

It is entirely up to you whether you want to receive this awesome gift from God. There are times, like with me, that the power of God will fall and you will receive the Baptism of the Holy Spirit supernaturally. Others receive by standing in a prayer line and having hands laid on them. There are others who receive by saying a simple prayer. When you asked for salvation, you received it by faith. When you ask for the Baptism of the Holy Spirit, you also receive it by faith.

If you would like to receive the Baptism, I will ask you to pray this prayer:

> Father, I ask you in the name of Jesus, to baptize me in the Holy Spirit. I have prayed in faith and believe that I have received.

If you prayed that prayer in sincerity, God just filled you with His Holy Spirit. You may now pray in your new prayer language. In my experience, some people receive their prayer language instantly. With others it may come in time, but it will come. Just keep praying and God will honor your prayer.

ENDORSEMENTS

Melda and I have known Jeanette and husband, Gary, for many years and have witnessed many lives transformed by their testimony. *The Warrior Inside* is a biography of Jeanette's life and how God's love, grace, and mercy prevail over evil. This story is about a young girl with no hope, born into a lifestyle of abuse and lawbreaking to survive in a very evil generation and season of her life. With sexual abuse, verbal and emotional abuse, as well as physical abuse from family members, Jeanette's early childhood set her on a course for destruction and even potential death. God knew all these evil circumstances would eventually be used to glorify Him one day. God knew Jennette would eventually give her life to Him, making Jesus her Lord and Savior and telling the story how God brought her through a time in the wilderness to a life blessed with abundance and assurance of knowing how much God loves her.

The Warrior Inside is a must-read for any age group. Youth to adult will enjoy reading and seeing how God took a young girl from poverty, lawlessness, and abuse to making her a daughter of the Most-High God. Jeanette's story is a true rags-to-riches story and provides all the drama, suspense, and surprise that will capture your attention. Once you begin reading, you will not be able to put it down. Jeanette's story will encourage you and bless you as you see a true miracle unfold before your eyes.

—David and Melda Bartholdi
Teachers and evangelists
Mark 16:15–20 International Ministries Inc.
www.onlybelieveGod.com

Jeanette Golden is a dedicate wife, mother, and now grandmother who has dedicated her life to Jesus. Her book of how God intervened in her life in a powerful, supernatural way will encourage and inspire you to know that with God all things are possible! It demonstrates not only the power of God but also His willingness to bring you from defeat to victory when you put your trust in Him.

I have had the privilege of being Jeanette's pastor for many years. She is a dedicated teacher, an able preacher, and a very powerful prayer warrior. I highly recommend her book as a must-read!

—Pastor Frank Ebarb
Word of Truth Family Church
Many, Louisiana

It is my great privilege to recommend to you Jeanette Golden's book. I have known her for twenty plus years and served with her in Aglow International. She truly has a servant's heart.

Jeanette is a powerful woman of faith, prayer, and the word. She is a dynamic, leader, visionary, teacher, speaker and author. Her sense of humor is contagious and refreshing. Anyone reading her book will be amazed at the honesty, hope and faith in Jeanette's life. As an encourager and lover of God and people, she has opened her heart to the world.

—Carol Torrance
US regional director, Aglow International

Of course, it goes without saying that I write this endorsement of *The Warrior Inside* with a bit of prejudice. Jeanette is my wife, my sweetheart, and I love her with all of my heart.

I can truly say that every word of this book is a true disclosure of God's mercy and grace in Jeanette's life. It is a love story written by the hand of God. It is also a story of a young girl who fought her way out of the pits of hell. Jeanette is my hero, my encourager, and my helpmate in every sense of the word. My prayer is that this book serves as a faith builder and guide to everyone who has lived a life of hurt and pain.

I love you, honey.

—Dr. Gary Golden

Mom told my brothers and me about her childhood when we were old enough to understand. It wasn't easy to think of how our mom had been treated by her own family. We, of course, had never been exposed to that type of lifestyle. As children, we were treated completely the opposite. Mom and Dad showed us nothing but love and kindness. Mom devoted her time to our dad, my brothers, and me. She was always there no matter what. If you needed her, all you had to do was call and she'd be there with open arms. She was also a powerful prayer warrior. If she couldn't handle our problems, she knew God could and would.

Mom wanted to make certain we grew up knowing about the love of Jesus and the sacrifice He made for us. She preached to us every time we got in a car or any chance she got. She taught us how to have a personal relationship with our Heavenly Father. At times we were a little overwhelmed by her constant preaching, but the teachings were things we needed to hear and understand. Later on we were able to instill those same principles into the lives of our children.

My brothers and I are very aware that God delivered my mom from what could have been a miserable, horrible life, or even physical death. He was her savior in every way. I hope Mom's life story blesses you as much as she has been a blessing to us.

—Andrew Golden

Jeanette's story is hope to the hopeless. It shows not only can you live this life and survive but you can live it and have victory in it. She became my sister in our early teens but has since become my mentor. Thank you, Jeanette, for teaching me just how good our God is. Love you, sis!

—Terri

This is a must read! Once you start reading, you won't be able to put it down. Jeanette joined our family as a young teenager, and we loved her from day one. It is nothing short of a miracle that she overcame the only life she knew, but God had great and wonderful plans for her, and He is not finished with her yet.

—Aunt Sandra Kurtz

ABOUT THE AUTHOR

Jeanette Golden's younger years were plagued with abuse, homelessness, and numerous heartaches. Her success in life mirrors the divine intervention of God and Jeanette's courageous efforts to overcome, bringing her to the place where she is today.

In her senior year at Richland High School, Jeanette was nominated and selected as a Who's Who in America's High School Students. She attended Stephen F. Austin State University in Nacogdoches, Texas, earning a Bachelor of Science Degree with a lifetime All-Level Certificate in Physical Education and a lifetime All-Level Certificate in Generic Special Education. Although retired from teaching, she maintains her love for sports and athleticism.

While in school she met and married Gary Golden, Doctor of Optometry. Jeanette and Gary reside in Hemphill, Texas, and are the proud parents of three sons and three grandchildren.

Jeanette has served as the president of the Hemphill Chapter of Women's Aglow International and President of the Optimist Club in Center, Texas. At present, she serves on the Board of Directors for Louie's Pizza and Prayer, Inc. Together, she and Gary serve on the Board of Directors/ Elders for Mark 16:15-20 International Ministries, Inc. From 2012 through 2014 Gary and Jeanette were pastors of Word of Truth Family Church in Hemphill, Texas. Jeanette remains active in both community and church activities. Jeanette's heart's cry is to reach the lost and hurting.

Jeanette's contact information: jgolden008@yahoo.com

CPSIA information can be obtained
at www.ICGtesting.com
Printed in the USA
LVHW032227220419
615089LV00005B/516